MW01687866

JAVASCRIPT

Quick Reference Guide

by Marc Miyashiro

ASP, Inc.
PO Box 23837
San Jose, California 95131, USA
(800) 777-UNIX

ISBN 0-935739-28-9

NOTICE

OTHER PUBLICATIONS AND SERVICES

ASP offers a full line of technical reference manuals, guides, and quick reference cards for UNIX, C/C++, Internet, and other topics. They are specifically designed for the professional who needs easy-to-access reference information to increase productivity. Please call or email (**books@aspinc.com**) for more information.

Korn Shell User and Programming Manual
UNIX Quick Reference Guide
C Shell Quick Reference Guide
Bourne Shell Quick Reference Guide
Korn Shell Quick Reference
Tcl Quick Reference Guide
Quick Reference Cards for Vi, C, C++, SCCS, HTML

CONVENTIONS

Keywords are shown in **bold** and should be typed exactly as given. Items in *italics* represent values that are to be substituted. Optional items are shown in [brackets].

OVERVIEW

CONTENTS

INTRODUCTION

This guide is designed as a reference and learning tool for JavaScript programmers and web developers. Users should have a general understanding of the Internet and the World Wide Web (WWW), as well as a good working knowledge of HyperText Markup Language (HTML).

JavaScript is a cross-platform, object-based scripting language developed by Netscape. The core language corresponds to **ECMA-262**, the scripting language endorsed by the European standards body, with some additions. It contains a set of core objects and additional objects that are specific to client and server versions.

> **Client-side JavaScript** is embedded directly in HTML pages and interpreted by the browser at runtime. Client specific objects include **window** and **history**.
>
> **Server-side JavaScript** is also embedded in HTML pages, but applications are compiled into bytecode executable files which are run in concert with a web server that contains the JavaScript runtime engine. Server-specific objects include **server** and **database**.

In addition to objects, JavaScript defines **operators**, **expressions**, **statements**, **functions**, **methods**, **events**, and **event handlers**.

> **Statement:** keywords used with appropriate syntax
>
> **Function:** a JavaScript procedure: a set of statements that performs a specific task
>
> **Method:** a function associated with an object
>
> **Event:** an action that occurs (usually as a result of something the user does)
>
> **Event Handlers:** a JavaScript function or series of statements which handles an event

JAVASCRIPT OPERATORS

ASSIGNMENT OPERATORS

An assignment operator assigns a value to its left operand based on the value of it right operand. For example, x += y means x = x+y

OPERATOR	DESCRIPTION
=	assigns the value of the second operand to the first
+=	adds two numbers and assigns the result to the first
-=	subtracts two numbers and assigns result to the first
*=	multiplies two numbers and assigns result to first
/=	divides two numbers and assigns result to the first
%=	computes the modulus of two numbers and assigns the result to the first
&=	performs a bitwise AND and assigns the result to the first operand
^=	performs a bitwise XOR and assigns the result to the first operand
|=	performs a bitwise OR and assigns the result to the first operand
<<=	performs a left shift and assigns the result to the first operand
>>=	performs a sign-propagating right shift and assigns the result to the first operand
>>>=	performs a zero-fill right shift and assigns the result to the first operand

ARITHMETIC OPERATORS

An arithmetic operator takes numerical values (either literals or variables) as operands and returns a single numerical value.

+	Addition: adds two numbers
++	Increment: adds 1 to a variable representing a number and returns either the new or old value of the variable
-	Negation: as a unary operator, negates the value of its argument Subtraction: as a binary operator, subtracts two numbers
—	Decrement: subtracts 1 from a variable representing a number and returns either the new or old value of the variable
*	Multiplication: multiplies two numbers
/	Division: divides two numbers
%	Modulus: computes the integer remainder after dividing two numbers

COMPARISON OPERATORS

A comparison operator compares its operands and returns a logical value based on whether the comparison is true or not. Operands can be numerical or string values. When used on string values, the comparisons are based on standard lexicographical ordering.

==	Equal: returns true if the operands are equal
!=	Not equal: returns true if the operands are not equal
>	Greater than: returns true if the left operand is greater than the right operand
>=	Greater than or equal: returns true if the left operand is greater than or equal to the right operand
<	Less than: returns true if the left operand is less than the right operand
<=	Less than or equal: returns true if the left operand is less than or equal to the right operand

BITWISE OPERATORS

A bitwise operator treats its operands as a set of bits (0s and 1s) rather than decimal, hexadecimal, or octal numbers. Although bitwise operators perform their operations on such binary representations, they return standard JavaScript numerical values

& Bitwise AND: returns a 1 in each bit position if bits of both operands are 1s

^ Bitwise XOR: returns a 1 in a bit position if bits of one but not both operands are 1

| Bitwise OR: returns a 1 in a bit if bits of either operand are 1

~ Bitwise NOT: flips the bits of its operand

<< Left Shift: shifts its first operand in binary representation to the left by the number of bits specified in the second operand, shifting in 0s from the right

>> Sign-propagating Right Shift: shifts the binary representation of the first operand to right by the number of bits specified in the second operands, discarding bits shifted off

>>> Zero-fill Right Shift: shifts the binary representation of the first operand to the right by the number of bits specified in the second operand, discarding bits shifted off, and shifting in 0s from the left.

LOGICAL OPERATORS

A logical operator takes Boolean (logical) values as operands and returns a Boolean value.

&& Logical AND: returns true if both logical operands are true; otherwise returns false

|| Logical OR: returns true if either logical expression is true; if both are false, returns false

! Logical Negation: returns false if its single operand is true; otherwise returns true

STRING OPERATORS

In addition to comparison operators, which can be used on string values, these operators are used to concatenate strings.

+	String Addition: concatenates two strings
+=	concatenates two strings and assigns the result to the first operand

SPECIAL OPERATORS

?: Conditional: lets you perform a simple "if...then...else";
the only JavaScript operator that takes 3 operands

SYNTAX: *condition* **?** *expr1* : *expr2*

PARAMETERS *condition:* an expresssion that evaluates to true or false

expr1, *expr2:* expressions with values of any type

, Comma: evaluates two expressions and returns the result of the second expression

SYNTAX: *expr1***,** *expr2*

PARAMETERS *expr1*, *expr2:* expressions with values of any type

delete delete: lets you delete an object property or an element at a specified index in an array

SYNTAX: **delete** *objectName.property*

delete *objectName*[*index*]

delete *property*

PARAMETERS *objectName:* the name of an object

property: an existing property

index: an integer representing the location of an element in an array

new

new: lets you create an instance of a user-defined object type or of one of the built-in object types

SYNTAX: *objectName* = **new** *objectType* (*param1* [,*param2*] ...[,*paramN*])

ARGUMENTS: *objectName:* name of the new object instance

objectType: must be a function that defines an object type

param1...paramN: property values for the object; these properties are parameters defined for the objectType function

this

this: keyword that you can use to refer to the current object

SYNTAX: **this**[.*propertyName*]

typeof

typeof: returns a string indicating the type of the unevaluated operand

SYNTAX: **typeof** operand

typeof (operand)

void

void: specifies an expression to be evaluated without returning a value

SYNTAX: javascript:**void** (*expression*)

javascript:**void** *expression*

KEYWORDS

JavaScript statements consist of keywords used with the appropriate syntax. A single statement may span multiple lines. Multiple statements may occur on a single line if each statement is separated by a semicolon.

SYNTAX CONVENTIONS: All keywords in syntax statements are in **bold**. Words in *italics* represent user-defined names or statements. Any portions enclosed in square brackets [ ] are optional. {statements} indicates a block of statements, which can consist of a single statement or multiple statements delimited by curly braces {}.

break terminates the current while or for loop and transfers program control to the statement following the terminated loop

SYNTAX **break**
break *label*

ARGUMENT *label:* identifier associated with the label of the statement

comment notations by the author to explain what a script does; comments are ignored by the interpreter

SYNTAX // comment text
/* multiple line comment text */

continue terminates execution of the block of statements in a while or for loop; continues execution of the loop with the next iteration

SYNTAX **continue**
continue *label*

ARGUMENT *label:* identifier associated with the label of the statement

delete deletes object's property or element of an array

SYNTAX **delete** *objectName.property*
delete *objectName*[*index*]
delete *property*

ARGUMENTS *objectName*: the name of an object
property: an existing property
index: an integer representing the location of an element in an array

do...while executes its statements until the test condition evaluates to false; statement is executed at least once

SYNTAX **do** *statement* **while** (*condition*);

ARGUMENTS *statement*: block of statements that is executed at least once and is re-executed each time the condition evaluates to true

condition: evaluated after each pass through the loop; if condition evaluates to true, the statements in the preceding block are re-executed; when condition evaluates to false, control passes to the statement following **do...while**

export allows a signed script to provide properties, functions, and objects to other signed or unsigned scripts

SYNTAX **export** *name1, name2, ..., nameN*
export *

ARGUMENTS *nameN*: list of properties, functions, and objects to be exported

*: exports all properties, functions, and objects from the script

for creates a loop that consists of three optional expressions enclosed in parentheses and separated by semicolons, followed by a block of statements executed in the loop

SYNTAX **for** ([*initial-expression*;] [*condition*;] [*increment-expression*]) { *statements* }

ARGUMENTS *initial-expression*: statement or variable declaration; typically used to initialize a counter variable; this expression may optionally declare new variables with the **var** keyword

condition: evaluated on each pass through the loop; if this condition evaluates to true, the statements in statements are performed; if this optional conditional test is omitted, the conditional always evaluates to true

increment-expression: generally used to update or increment the counter variable *statements:* block of statements that are executed as long as condition evaluates to true; single or multiple statements; although not required, it is good practice to indent these statements from the beginning of the for statement

for...in iterates a specified variable over all the properties of an object; for each distinct property, JavaScript executes the specified statements

SYNTAX: **for** (*variable* in *object*) {*statements*}

ARGUMENTS: *variable:* variable to iterate over every property object
object: object for which the properties are iterated
statements: block of statements executed for each property

function declares a JavaScript function name with the specified parameters; acceptable parameters include strings, numbers, and objects

SYNTAX: **function** *name*([*param*] [, *param*] [..., *param*]) {*statements*}

ARGUMENTS: *name:* the function name
param: the name of an argument to be passed to the function; a function can have up to 255 arguments

if...else executes a set of statements if a specified condition is true; if the condition is false, another set of statements can be executed

SYNTAX: **if** (*condition*) { *statements1*} [**else** { *statements2*}]

ARGUMENTS: *condition:* can be any JavaScript expression that evaluates to true or false; parentheses are required around the condition; if the condition evaluates to true, the statements in *statements1* are executed
statements1 statements2 can be any JavaScript statements, including further nested **if** statements; multiple statements must be enclosed in braces

import allows a script to import properties, functions, and objects from a signed script which has exported the information

SYNTAX: **import** *objectName.name1, objectName.name2, ..., objectName.nameN*
import *objectName.**

ARGUMENTS: *nameN:* list of properties, functions, and objects to import from the export file
objectName: name of the object that will receive the imported names
*: imports all properties, functions, and objects from the export script

label provides an identifier that can be used with **break** or **continue** to indicate where the program should continue

SYNTAX: **label** : *statement*

ARGUMENTS: *statement:* block of statements; **break** can be used with any labeled statement; **continue** can be used with looping labeled statements

return specifies the value to be returned by a function

SYNTAX: **return** *expression*

switch allows a program to evaluate an expression and attempt to match the expression's value to a case label

SYNTAX: **switch** (*expression*) { case label : *statement*; **break**; case label : *statement*; **break**; ... default : *statement*; }

var declares a variable, optionally initializing it to a value

SYNTAX: **var** *varname* [= *value*] [..., *varname* [= *value*]]

ARGUMENTS: *varname:* variable name; can be any legal identifier
value: initial value of the variable; can be any legal expression

while creates a loop that evaluates an expression; if it is true, it executes a block of statements

SYNTAX: **while** (*condition*) { *statements* }

ARGUMENTS: *condition* : evaluated before each pass through the loop; if the condition evaluates to true, the statements in the succeeding block are performed; when the condition evaluates to false, execution continues with the statement following statements

statements : block of statements that are executed as long as the condition evaluates to true; although not required, it is good practice to indent these statements from the beginning of the statement

with establishes the default object for a set of statements

SYNTAX: **with** (*object*) { *statements* }

ARGUMENTS: *object* : specifies the default object to use for the statements; the parentheses around object are required

statements : any block of statements

FUNCTIONS

A **function** is a JavaScript procedure: a set of statements that performs a specific task.

Functions are *defined* within scripts *in the head* and *called* within scripts *in the body. Defining* the function simply names the function and specifies what to do when the function is called. *Calling* the function performs the specified actions with the indicated parameters.

DEFINING FUNCTIONS

SYNTAX:

function *functionName(arg1,arg2,arg3...)* {*statements*}

The basic elements are:

The **function** keyword, a function name (with a comma-separated list of arguments to the function in parentheses), and the statements in the function in curly braces.

The predefined Function object specifies a string of JavaScript code to be compiled as a function. To create a Function object:

functionObjectName = new Function ([*arg1, arg2, ... argn*], *functionBody*)

Function objects are evaluated each time they are used. This is less efficient than *declaring* a function and *calling* it within your code, because declared functions are compiled.

CALLING FUNCTIONS

Defining a function does not execute it. You have to *call* the function for it to do its work. For example, if you define a function called sample_function in the HEAD of the document, you can call it with the following script:

```
<SCRIPT>
sample_function("argument")
</SCRIPT>
```

The arguments of a function are not limited to strings and numbers. You can pass whole objects to a function, too. A function can even be recursive, that is, it can call itself.

In Navigator 4.0, you can nest a function within a function. (In technical terms, JavaScript now supports lambda expressions and lexical closures.) The nested function can use the arguments and variables of the outer function. The outer function cannot use the arguments and variables of the nested function.

USING THE ARGUMENTS ARRAY

The arguments of a function are maintained in an array. Within a function, you can address the parameters passed to it as follows:

functionName.arguments[*i*]

where *functionName* is the name of the function and *i* is the ordinal number of the argument, starting at zero.

The total number of arguments is indicated by the variable **arguments.length**.

If you don't know in advance how many arguments will be passed to the function, use the arguments array to call a function with more arguments than it is formally declared to accept. You can use **arguments.length** to determine the number of arguments actually passed to the function, and then treat each argument using the arguments array.

For example, consider a function defined to create HTML lists. The only formal argument for the function is a string that is "U" for an unordered (bulleted) list or "O" for an ordered (numbered) list. The function is defined as follows:

```
function list(type) {
   document.write("<" + type + "L>") // begin list
   // iterate through arguments
   for (var i = 1; i < list.arguments.length; i++)
      document.write("<LI>" + list.arguments[i])
      document.write("</" + type + "L>") // end list
}
```

You can pass any number of arguments to this function, and it will then display each argument as an item in the indicated type of list. For example, the following call to the function

```
list("o", "apples", "bananas", 3.1418, "and so on...")
```

results in this output:

1. apples
2. bananas
3. 3.1418
4. and so on...

In addition to a list of indexed elements and a length property, arguments include these additional properties in JavaScript 1.2:

- formal arguments: each formal argument of a function is a property of the arguments array.
- local variables: each local variable of a function is a property of the arguments array.
- caller: a property whose value is the arguments array of the outer function. If there is no outer function, the value is undefined.
- callee: a property whose value is the function reference.

ASSOCIATED OBJECTS

A **method** is a function associated with an object. Methods are described under their associated objects on pages 43-131. See page 132 for an alphabetical listing of methods to identify the objects with which they are associated.

The following section describes predefined functions which are not associated with any object. These are called **global functions**.

GLOBAL FUNCTIONS

These functions are not associated with any specific object. Each definition specifies whether the function operates on the client-side, server-side, or both (core functions). The definition also indicates the earliest version of Netscape client or server software which supports the function.

addClient

Adds client object property values to a dynamically generated URL or the URL used with the redirect function. Server-side function. LiveWire 1.0

see also:
redirect
page 29

SYNTAX: addClient(***URL***)

PARAMETER:

URL A string representing a URL

DESCRIPTION

The addClient function is a top-level server-side JavaScript function.

Use addClient to preserve client object property values when you use **redirect** or generate dynamic links. This is necessary if an application uses client or server URL encoding to maintain the client object; it does no harm in other cases. Since the client maintenance technique can be changed after the application has been compiled, it is always safer to use addClient, even if you do not anticipate using a URL encoding scheme.

EXAMPLES:

Example 1. In the following example, addClient is used with the redirect function to redirect a browser:

```
redirect(addClient("mypage.html"))
```

Example 2. In the following example, addClient preserves client object property values when a link is dynamically generated:

```
<A HREF='addClient("page"" + project.pageno +
".html")'>Jump to new page</A>
```

addResponseHeader Adds new information to the response header sent to the client. Server-side function. Netscape Server 3.0

SYNTAX: addResponseHeader(*field, value*)

PARAMETERS

field A field to add to the response header.

value The information to specify for that field.

DESCRIPTION

You can use the addResponseHeader function to add custom content type or any other information you want to the response header.

Remember that the header is sent with the first part of the response. Therefore, you should call these functions early in the script on each page. In particular, you should ensure that the response header is set *before* any of these happen:

see also: deleteResponseHeader *page 18*

- The runtime engine generates 64KB of content for the HTML page (it automatically flushes the output buffer at this point).
- You call the **flush** function to clear the output buffer.
- You call the **redirect** function to change client requests.

EXAMPLES:

If the response you send to the client uses a custom content type, you should encode this content type in the response header. The JavaScript runtime engine automatically adds the default content type (text/html) to the response header. If you want a custom header, you must first remove the old default content type from the header and then add the new one. If your response uses royalairways-format as a custom content type, you would specify it this way:

deleteResponseHeader("content-type");

addResponseHeader("content-type", "royalairways-format");

blob

Assigns BLOb data to a column in a cursor. Server-side function. LiveWire 1.0

SYNTAX: blob (***path***)

PARAMETER:

path a string representing the name of a file containing BLOb data. This string must be an absolute pathname

RETURNS: a blob object

DESCRIPTION

Use this function with an updatable cursor to insert or update a row containing BLOb data. To insert or update a row using SQL and the execute method, use the syntax supported by your database vendor.

On DB2, blobs are limited to 32 KBytes.

Because back slash ("\") is the escape character in JavaScript, in NT filenames you must either use 2 backslashes or a forward slash.

EXAMPLE:

The following statements update BLOb data from the specified GIF files in columns HOUSE and CAR of the current row of the RESIDENT table.

```
// Create a cursor
cursor = database.cursor("SELECT * FROM customer
    WHERE customer.ID = " + request.customerID)
// Position the pointer on the row
cursor.next()
// Assign the blob data
cursor.house = blob("c:/customer/photos/myhouse.gif")
cursor.car = blob("c:/customer/photos/mycar.gif")
// And update the row
cursor.updateRow("resident")
```

callC

Calls an external function and returns the value returned by the external function. Server-side function. LiveWire 1.0

SYNTAX: callC(***JSFunctionName, arg1,..., argN***)

PARAMETERS

JSFunctionName the name of the function as it is identified with RegisterCFunction

arg1...argN a comma-separated list of arguments to the external function; the arguments can be any JavaScript values: strings, numbers, or Boolean values. The number of arguments must match the number of arguments required by the external function.

see also:
registerCFunction
page 30

DESCRIPTION

The callC function is a top-level server-side JavaScript function.

The callC function returns the string value that the external function returns; callC can only return string values.

EXAMPLE:

The following example assigns a value to the variable isRegistered according to whether the attempt to register the external function echoCCallArguments succeeds or fails. If isRegistered is true, the callC function executes.

```
var isRegistered =
    registerCFunction("echoCCallArguments",
        "c:/mypath/mystuff.dll",
        "mystuff_EchoCCallArguments")
if (isRegistered == true) {
    var returnValue =
    callC("echoCCallArguments", "first arg", 42, true, "last arg")
    write(returnValue)
}
```

debug Displays a JavaScript expression in the trace facility. Server-side function. LiveWire 1.0

SYNTAX: debug(***expression***)

PARAMETERS

expression any valid JavaScript expression

DESCRIPTION

The debug function is a top-level server-side JavaScript function that displays the value of an expression for debugging purposes. The value is displayed in the trace facility of the Application Manager following the label "Debug message:".

EXAMPLE:

The following example displays the value of the variable *data*:

debug("The final value of data is " + *data*)

deleteResponseHeader Removes information from the header of the response sent to the client. Server-side function. Netscape Server 3.0

SYNTAX: deleteResponseHeader(***field***)

PARAMETERS

field a field to remove from the response header

DESCRIPTION

You can use the deleteResponseHeader function to remove information from the header of the response you send to the client. The most frequent use of this function is to remove the default content-type information before adding your own content-type information with addResponseHeader .

see also: addResponseHeader *page 15*

escape

Returns the hexadecimal encoding of an argument in the ISO-Latin-1 character set. Core function. Navigator 2.0, LiveWire 1.0

SYNTAX: escape("***string***")

PARAMETERS

string a string in the ISO-Latin-1 character set

DESCRIPTION

The escape function is a top-level JavaScript function which encodes special characters in the specified string and returns the new string. It encodes spaces, punctuation, and any other character that is not an ASCII alphanumeric character, with the exception of these characters:

see also: unescape *page 36*

* @ - _ + . /

Use the escape and unescape functions to add property values manually to a URL.

EXAMPLES:

Example 1. The following example returns "%26":

```
escape("&")
```

Example 2. This statement

```
escape("The_rain. In Spain, Ma'am")
```

returns

"The_rain.%20In%20Spain%2C%20Ma%92am"

Example 3. In the following example, the value of the variable theValue is encoded as a hexadecimal string and passed on to the request object when a user clicks the link:

```
<A HREF=\Q"mypage.html?val1="+escape(theValue)\Q)>
Click Here</A>
```

eval

Evaluates a string of JavaScript code without reference to a particular object.
Core function. Navigator 2.0

SYNTAX: eval(***string***)

PARAMETERS;

string a string representing a JavaScript expression, statement, or sequence of statements; the expression can include variables and properties of existing objects

DESCRIPTION

The argument of the eval function is a string. If the string represents an expression, eval evaluates the expression. If the argument represents one or more JavaScript statements, eval performs the statements. *Do not* call eval to evaluate an arithmetic expression; JavaScript evaluates arithmetic expressions automatically.

If you construct an arithmetic expression as a string, you can use eval to evaluate it at a later time. For example, for variable x, you can postpone evaluation of an expression involving x by assigning the string value of the expression, say "3 * x + 2", to a variable, and then calling eval at a later point in your script.

eval is also a method of all objects. This method is described for the Object class.

EXAMPLES:

The following examples display output using **document.write**. In server-side JavaScript, you can display the same output by calling the **write** function instead of using **document.write**.

Example 1. Both of the write statements below display 42. The first evaluates the string "x + y + 1"; the second evaluates the string "42".

```
var x = 2
var y = 39
var z = "42"
document.write(eval("x + y + 1"), "<BR>")
   document.write(eval(z), "<BR>")
```

Example 2. In the following example, the getFieldName(n) function returns the name of the specified form element as a string. The first statement assigns the string value of the third form element to the variable field. The second statement uses eval to display the value of the form element.

```
var field = getFieldName(3)
document.write("The field named ", field, " has value of ",
eval(field + ".value"))
```

Example 3. The following example uses eval to evaluate the string str. This string consists of JavaScript statements that open an Alert dialog box and assign z a value of 42 if x is five, and assigns 0 to z otherwise. When the second statement is executed, eval will cause these statements to be performed, and it will also evaluate the set of statements and return the value that is assigned to z.

```
var str = "if (x == 5) {alert('z is 42'); z = 42;} else z = 0; "
document.write("<P>z is ", eval(str))
```

Example 4. In the following example, the setValue function uses eval to assign the value of the variable newValue to the text field

```
textObject:
function setValue (textObject, newValue) {
eval ("document.forms[0]." + textObject + ".value") =
newValue
}
```

Example 5. The following example creates model as a property of the object myCar, and also as a variable. The first write statement uses eval('model') without specifying an object; the string "model" is evaluated without regard to any object, and the write method displays "Civic", which is the value of the model variable. The second write statement uses myCar.eval('model') which specifies the object myCar; the string "model" is evaluated with regard to the myCar object, and the write method displays "Accord", which is the value of the make property of the myCar object.

```
function Car(make,model,color) {
     this.make=make
     this.model=model
     this.color=color
}
myCar = new Car("Honda")
myCar.model="Accord"
var model="Civic"
document.write("<P>" + eval('model'))
document.write("<BR>" + myCar.eval('model'))
```

flush

Sends data from the internal buffer to the client. Server-side function. LiveWire 1.0

SYNTAX: flush()

PARAMETERS **none**

DESCRIPTION

To improve performance, JavaScript buffers the HTML page it constructs. The flush function immediately sends data from the internal buffer to the client. If you do not explicitly call the flush function, JavaScript sends data to the client after each 64KB of content in the constructed HTML page.

Use the flush function to control when data is sent to the client. For example, call the flush function before an operation that creates a delay, such as a database query. If a database query retrieves a large number of rows, you can flush the buffer after retrieving a small number of rows to prevent long delays in displaying data.

see also:
write
page 38

Because the flush function updates the client's cookie file as part of the HTTP header, you should perform any changes to the client object before flushing the buffer, if you are using client cookie to maintain the client object.

NOTE: Do not confuse the flush method of the File object with the top-level flush function, which is a server-side JavaScript function that is not associated with any object.

EXAMPLE:

The following example iterates through a text file and outputs each line in the file, preceded by a line number and five spaces. The flush function then causes the client to display the output.

```
while (!In.eof()) {
    AscLine = In.readln();
    if (!In.eof())
    write(LPad(LineCount + ": ", 5), AscLine, "\n");
    LineCount++;
    flush();
}
```

getOptionValue Returns the text of a selected OPTION in a SELECT form element. Server-side function. LiveWire 1.0

SYNTAX: getOptionValue(***name, index***)

PARAMETERS

name	a name specified by the NAME attribute of the <SELECT> tag
index	zero-based ordinal index of the selected option
Returns	a string containing the text for the selected option, as specified by the associated <OPTION> tag

DESCRIPTION

The getOptionValue function is a top-level server-side JavaScript function corresponding to the Option.text property available to client-side JavaScript.

see also:
getOptionValueCount
page 24

The <SELECT> tag allows multiple values to be associated with a single form element, with the MULTIPLE attribute. If your application requires select lists that allow multiple selected options, you use the getOptionValue function to get the values of selected options in server-side JavaScript.

EXAMPLE:

Suppose you have the following form element:

```
<SELECT NAME="Dinner Menu" MULTIPLE SIZE=8>
<OPTION SELECTED>Beef
        <OPTION>Chicken
        <OPTION>Fish
        <OPTION SELECTED>Rice
        <OPTION>Potatoes
        <OPTION SELECTED>Broccoli
        <OPTION>Carrots
        <OPTION>Zucchini
</SELECT>
```

You could process the input from this select list in server-side JavaScript as follows:

```
<SERVER> var loopIndex = 0
var loopCount = getOptionValueCount("Dinner Menu") // 3 by default
while ( loopIndex < loopCount ) {
    var optionValue = getOptionValue("Dinner Menu",loopIndex)
    write("<br>Item #" + loopIndex + ": " + optionValue + "\n")
    loopIndex++
}
</SERVER>
```

If the user kept the default selections, this script would return

Item #1: Beef Item #4: Rice Item #6: Broccoli

getOptionValueCount

Returns the number of options selected by the user in a SELECT form element. Server-side function, LiveWire 1.0

SYNTAX: getOptionValueCount(***name***)

PARAMETERS

name Specified by the NAME attribute of the <SELECT> tag.

DESCRIPTION

see also: getOptionValue *page 23*

The getOptionValueCount function is a top-level server-side JavaScript function (used with getOptionValue) to process user input from SELECT form elements that allow multiple selections.

EXAMPLE

See the example for getOptionValue, page 23.

isNaN

Evaluates an argument to determine if it is not a number. Core function. Navigator 2.0: Unix only; Navigator 3.0, LiveWire 1.0: all platforms

SYNTAX: isNaN(***testValue***)

PARAMETER:

testValue the value you want to evaluate

DESCRIPTION

isNaN is a built-in JavaScript function. It is not a

method associated with any object, but is part of the language itself.

see also:
Number
page 25
parseFloat
page 26
parseInt
page 27

On platforms that support NaN, the parseFloat and parseInt functions return "NaN" when they evaluate a value that is not a number. isNaN returns true if passed "NaN", and false otherwise.

EXAMPLE:

The following example evaluates floatValue to determine if it is a number and then calls a procedure accordingly:

```
floatValue=parseFloat(toFloat)
if (isNaN(floatValue)) {
        notFloat()
} else {
        isFloat()
}
```

Number

Converts the specified object to a number. Core function, Navigator 4.0, Netscape Server 3.0

SYNTAX: Number(***obj***)

PARAMETER:

obj An object

DESCRIPTION

When the object is a Date object, Number returns a value in milliseconds measured from 01 January, 1970 UTC (GMT), positive after this date, negative before.

If obj is a string that does not contain a well-formed numeric literal, Number returns NaN.

EXAMPLE:

The following example converts the Date object to a numerical value:

```
<SCRIPT> d = new Date ("December 17, 1995
03:24:00");
document.write (Number(d) + "<BR>");
</SCRIPT>
```

This prints "819199440000."

parseFloat Parses a string argument and returns a floating point number. Core function.

Navigator 2.0: If the first character of the string specified in parseFloat(string) cannot be converted to a number, returns "NaN" on Solaris and Irix and 0 on all other platforms.

Navigator 3.0, **LiveWire 1.0**: Returns "NaN" on all platforms if the first character of the string specified in parseFloat(string) cannot be converted to a number.

SYNTAX: parseFloat(***string***)

PARAMETERS

string a string that represents the value you want to parse

DESCRIPTION

The parseFloat function is a built-in JavaScript function that parses its argument (a string) and returns a floating point number. If it encounters a character other than a sign (+ or -), numeral (0-9), a decimal point, or an exponent, then it returns the value up to that point and ignores that character and all succeeding characters.

If the first character cannot be converted to a number, parseFloat returns "NaN".

For arithmetic purposes, the "NaN" value is not a number in any radix. You can call theisNaN function to determine if the result ofparseFloat is "NaN". If "NaN" is passed on to arithmetic operations, the operation results will also be "NaN".

see also:
isNaN
page 23
parseInt
page 27

EXAMPLES:

The following examples all return 3.14:

```
parseFloat("3.14")
parseFloat("314e-2")
parseFloat("0.0314E+2")
var x = "3.14" parseFloat(x)
```

The following example returns "NaN":

```
parseFloat("FF2")
```

parseInt Parses a string argument and returns an integer of the specified radix or base. Core function. **Navigator 2.0**: If the first character of the string specified in parseInt(string) cannot be converted to a number, returns "NaN" on Solaris and Irix and 0 on all other platforms. **Navigator 3.0**, **LiveWire 2.0**: Returns "NaN" on all platforms if the first character of the string specified in parseInt(string) cannot be converted to a number.

SYNTAX: parseInt(***string,radix***)

PARAMETERS

string a string that represents the value you want to parse

radix (optional) an integer that represents the radix (base) of the return value

DESCRIPTION

see also:
isNaN
page 23
parseFloat
page 26

The parseInt function is a built-in JavaScript function that parses its first argument (a string) and attempts to return an integer of the specified *radix* (base). For example, a *radix* of 10 indicates to convert to a decimal number, 8 = octal, 16 = hexadecimal, and so on. For radixes above 10, the letters of the alphabet indicate numerals greater than 9. For example, with hexadecimal numbers (base 16), A through F are used.

If parseInt encounters a character that is not a numeral in the specified radix, it ignores it and all succeeding characters and returns the integer value parsed up to that point. parseInt truncates numbers to integer values.

If the radix is not specified or is specified as 0, JavaScript assumes the following:

If the input string begins with "0x", the radix is 16 (hexadecimal).

If the input string begins with "0", the radix is eight (octal).

If the input string begins with any other value, the radix is 10 (decimal).

If the first character cannot be converted to a number, parseInt returns "NaN".

For arithmetic purposes, the "NaN" value is not a number in any radix. You can call the isNaN function to determine if the result of parseInt is "NaN". If "NaN" is passed on to arithmetic operations, the operation results will also be "NaN".

EXAMPLES:

The following examples all return 15:

```
parseInt("F", 16)
parseInt("17", 8)
parseInt("15", 10)
parseInt(15.99, 10)
parseInt("FXX123", 16)
parseInt("1111", 2)
parseInt("15*3", 10)
```

The following examples all return "NaN":

```
parseInt("Hello", 8)
parseInt("0x7", 10)
parseInt("FFF", 10)
```

Even though the radix is specified differently, the following examples all return 17 because the input string begins with "0x".

```
parseInt("0x11", 16)
parseInt("0x11", 0)
parseInt("0x11")
```

redirect

Redirects the client to the specified URL.
Server-side function. LiveWire 1.0

SYNTAX: redirect(***location***)

PARAMETER:

location The URL to which you want to redirect the client.

DESCRIPTION

The redirect function is a top-level server-side JavaScript function that redirects the client browser to the URL specified by the location parameter. The value of location can be relative or absolute.

When the client encounters a redirect function, it loads the specified page immediately and discards the current page. The client does not execute or load any HTML or script statements in the page following the redirect function.

see also:
addClient
page 14

You can use the addClient function to preserve client object property values. See addClient for more information.

EXAMPLE:

The following example uses the redirect function to redirect a client browser:

redirect("http://www.royalairways.com/lw/apps/newhome.html")

The page displayed by the newhome.html link could contain content such as the following:

<H1>New location</H1> The URL you tried to access has been moved to:

<A HREF=http://www.royalairways.com/lw/apps/index.html> http://www.royalairways.com/lw/apps/index.html</A>

<P>This notice will remain until 12/31/97.

registerCFunction Registers an external function for use with a server-side JavaScript application. Server-side function. LiveWire 1.0

SYNTAX: registerCFunction(***JSFunctionName, libraryPath, externalFunctionName***)

PARAMETERS

JSFunctionName the name of the function as it is called in JavaScript

libraryPath the full filename and path of the library, using the conventions of your operating system

externalFunctionName the name of the function as it is defined in the library

DESCRIPTION

registerCFunction is a top-level server-side JavaScript function that makes an external function available to a server-side JavaScript application. The function can be written in any language, but you must use C calling conventions.

To use an external function in a server-side JavaScript application, register the function with registerCFunction, and then call it with the callC function. Once an application registers a function, you can call the function any number of times.

see also:
callC
page 17

The registerCFunction function returns true if the external function is registered successfully; otherwise, it returns false. For example, registerCFunction can return false if the JavaScript runtime engine cannot find either the library or the specified function inside the library.

To use a backslash (\) character as a directory separator in the libraryPath parameter, you must enter a double backslash (\\). The single backslash is a reserved character.

EXAMPLE:

See the example for the callC function.

ssjs_generateClientID

Returns a unique string you can use to uniquely specify the client object. Server-side function, Netscape Server 3.0

SYNTAX: ssjs_generateClientID()

PARAMETERS: **none**

DESCRIPTION

see also:
ssjs_getClientID
page 33

This function is closely related to ssjs_getClientID. See the description of that function for information on these functions and the differences between them.

ssjs_getCGIVariable

Returns the value of the specified environment variable set in the server process, including some CGI variables. Server-side function, Netscape Server 3.0

SYNTAX: ssjs_getCGIVariable(***varName***)

PARAMETER:

varName A string containing the name of the environment variable to retrieve.

DESCRIPTION

ssjs_getCGIVariable lets you access the environment variables set in the server process, including the CGI variables listed below:

Variable	*Description*
AUTH_TYPE	The authorization type, if the request is protected by any type of authorization. Netscape web servers support HTTP basic access authorization. Example value: basic
HTTPS	If security is active on the server, the value of this variable is ON; otherwise, it is OFF. Example value: ON
HTTPS_KEYSIZE	The number of bits in the session key used to encrypt the session, if security is on. Example value: 128
HTTPS_SECRETKEYSIZE	The number of bits used to generate the server's private key. Example value: 128
PATH_INFO	Path information, as sent by the browser.

	Example value: /cgivars/cgivars.html
PATH_TRANSLATED	The actual system-specific pathname of the path contained in PATH_INFO. Example value: /usr/ns-home/myhttpd/js/samples/cgivars/cgivars.html
QUERY_STRING	Information from the requesting HTML page; if "?" is present, the information in the URL that comes after the "?". Example value: x=42
REMOTE_ADDR	The IP address of the host that submitted the request. Example value: 198.93.95.47
REMOTE_HOST	If DNS is turned on for the server, the name of the host that submitted the request; otherwise, its IP address. Example value: www.netscape.com
REMOTE_USER	The name of the local HTTP user of the web browser, if HTTP access authorization has been activated for this URL. Note that this is not a way to determine the user name of any person accessing your program. Example value: ksmith
REQUEST_METHOD	The HTTP method associated with the request. An application can use this to determine the proper response to a request. Example value: GET
SCRIPT_NAME	The pathname to this page, as it appears in the URL. Example value: cgivars.html
SERVER_NAME	The hostname or IP address on which the JavaScript application is running, as it appears in the URL. Example value: piccolo.mcom.com
SERVER_PORT	The TCP port on which the server is running. Example value: 2020
SERVER_PROTOCOL	The HTTP protocol level supported by the client's software. Example value: HTTP/1.0
SERVER_URL	The URL that the user typed to access this server. Example value: https://piccolo:2020

If you supply an argument that isn't one of the CGI variables listed, the runtime engine looks for an environment variable by that name in the server environment. If found, the runtime engine returns the value; otherwise, it returns null. For example, the following code assigns the value of the standard CLASSPATH environment variable to the JavaScript variable classpath:

```
classpath = ssjs_getCGIVariable("CLASSPATH");
```

ssjs_getClientID Returns the identifier for the client object used by some of JavaScript's client-maintenance techniques. Server-side function. Netscape Server 3.0

SYNTAX: ssjs_getClientID()

PARAMETERS: **none**

DESCRIPTION

For some applications, you may want to store information specific to a client/application pair in the project or server objects. In these situations, you need a way to refer uniquely to the client/application pair. JavaScript provides two functions for this purpose, ssjs_generateClientID and ssjs_getClientID.

see also:
ssjs_generateClientID
page 32

Each time you call ssjs_generateClientID, the runtime engine returns a new identifier. For this reason, if you use this function and want the identifier to last longer than a single client request, you need to store the identifier, possibly as a property of the client object. If you use this function and store the ID in the client object, be careful that an intruder cannot get access to that ID and hence to sensitive information.

An alternative approach uses the ssjs_getClientID function. If you use one of the server-side maintenance techniques for the client object, the JavaScript runtime engine generates and uses an identifier to access the information for a particular client/application pair. ssjs_getClientID returns the identifier used by the runtime engine. Every time you call this function from a particular client/application pair, you get the same identifier. Therefore, you do not need to store the identifier returned by ssjs_getClientID.

However, if you use any of the other maintenance techniques, this function returns "undefined"; if you use those techniques you must instead use the ssjs_generateClientID function. If you use a client-side maintenance technique, you cannot use the ssjs_getClientID function; you must use the ssjs_generateClientID function.

String

Converts the specified object to a string.

Core function. Navigator 4.0, Netscape Server 3.0

SYNTAX: String(***obj***)

PARAMETER:

obj an object

DESCRIPTION

When the object is a Date object, String returns a string representation of the date. Its format is:
Thu Aug 18 04:37:43 Pacific Daylight Time 1983.

EXAMPLE:

The following example converts the Date object to a readable string.

```
<SCRIPT> D = new Date (430054663215);
document.write (String(D) +" <BR>");
</SCRIPT>
```

This prints "Thu Aug 18 04:37:43 Pacific Daylight Time 1983."

taint

Adds tainting to a data element or script.
Core function, Navigator 3.0;
removed in Navigator 4.0

SYNTAX : taint(***dataElementName***)

PARAMETER:

dataElementName (optional) the property, variable, function, or object to taint. If omitted, taint is added to the script itself

DESCRIPTION

Tainting prevents other scripts from passing information that should be secure and private, such as directory structures or user session history. JavaScript cannot pass tainted values on to any server without the end user's permission.

Use taint to mark data that otherwise is not tainted.

In some cases, control flow rather than data flow carries tainted information. In these cases, taint is added to the script's window. You can add taint to the script's window by calling taint with no arguments.

taint does not modify its argument; instead, it returns a marked copy of the value, or, for objects, an unmarked reference to the value.

EXAMPLE:

The following statement adds taint to a property so that a script cannot send it to another server without the end user's permission:

```
taintedStatus=taint(window.defaultStatus)
        // taintedStatus now cannot be sent
        // in a URL or form post without
        // the end user's permission
```

unescape Returns the ASCII string for the specified value. Core function. Navigator 2.0

SYNTAX: unescape(***string***)

PARAMETER:

string a string containing characters in the form "%xx", where xx is a 2-digit hexadecimal number

DESCRIPTION

see also:
escape
page 19

The string returned by the unescape function is a series of characters in the ISO-Latin-1 character set. The unescape function is a top-level JavaScript function not associated with any object. In server-side JavaScript, use this function to decode name/value pairs in URLs.

EXAMPLES:

The following client-side example returns "&":

unescape("%26")

The following client-side example returns "!#":

unescape("%21%23")

In the following server-side example, val1 has been passed to the request object as a hexadecimal value. The statement assigns the decoded value of val1 to myValue.

myValue = **unescape**(**request**.*val1*)

untaint

Removes tainting from a data element or script. Core function, Navigator 3.0; removed in Navigator 4.0

SYNTAX: untaint(***dataElementName***)

PARAMETER:

dataElementName (optional) the property, variable, function, or object to remove tainting from. If omitted, taint is removed from the script itself.

DESCRIPTION

Tainting prevents other scripts from passing information that should be secure and private, such as directory structures or user session history. JavaScript cannot pass tainted values on to any server without the end user's permission.

Use untaint to clear tainting that marks data that should not to be sent by other scripts to different servers.

A script can untaint only data that originated in that script (that is, only data that has the script's taint code or has the identity (null) taint code). If you use untaint with a data element from another server's script (or any data that you cannot untaint), untaint returns the data without change or error.

In some cases, control flow rather than data flow carries tainted information. In these cases, taint is added to the script's window. You can remove taint from the script's window by calling untaint with no arguments, if the window contains taint only from the current window.

untaint does not modify its argument; instead, it returns an unmarked copy of the value, or, for objects, an unmarked reference to the value.

EXAMPLE:

The following statement removes taint from a property so that a script can send it to another server:

```
untaintedStatus=untaint(window.defaultStatus)
            // untaintedStatus can now be sent
            // in a URL or form post by other
            // scripts
```

write

Generates HTML based on an expression and sends it to the client. Server-side function. LiveWire 1.0

SYNTAX: write(***expression***)

PARAMETER:

expression a valid JavaScript expression

DESCRIPTION

The write function is a top-level server-side JavaScript function that causes server-side JavaScript to generate HTML that is sent to the client. The client interprets this generated HTML as it would static HTML. The server-side write function is similar to the client-side document.write method.

see also:
flush
page 22

To improve performance, the JavaScript engine on the server buffers the output to be sent to the client and sends it in large blocks of at most 64 KBytes in size. You can control when data are sent to the client by using the flush function.

NOTE: Do not confuse the write method of the File object with the write function. The write function outputs data to the client; the write method outputs data to a physical file on the server.

EXAMPLE:

In the following example, the write function is passed a string, concatenated with a variable, concatenated with a <BR> tag:

```
write("The operation returned " + returnValue + "<BR>")
```

If returnValue is 57, this example displays the following:

The operation returned 57

JAVASCRIPT OBJECTS

JavaScript is based on a simple object-oriented paradigm. An object is a construct with *properties* that may be JavaScript variables or other objects. An object may have *functions* associated with it; these are known as the object's *methods.*

JavaScript has a number of predefined objects. Core objects are defined for both client-side and server-side scripts and described on pages 43-53. Client-side objects are described on pages 54-105. Server-side objects are described on pages 106-131.

In addition, you can create your own objects.

CREATING NEW OBJECTS

In JavaScript 1.2, you can create objects using literal notation. The syntax for creating a literal object is:

```
objectName = {property1:value1,
property2:value2,..., propertyN:valueN}
```

where objectName is the name of the new object, each propertyI is an identifier (either a name, a number, or a string literal), and each valueI is an expression whose value is assigned to the propertyI.

If an object is created using literal notation in a top-level script, JavaScript interprets the object each time it evaluates the expression containing the object literal. In addition, a literal used in a function is created each time the function is called.

Alternatively, you can create your own object with these two steps:

1. Define the object type by writing a constructor function.
2. Create an instance of the object with **new**.

To define an object type, create a function for the object type that specifies its name, properties, and methods. For example:

```
function objectType(property1, property2) {
   this.property1 = property1
   this.method1 = method1
}
```

Notice the use of **this** (see page 42) to assign values to the object's properties and methods based on the values passed to the function.

Now you can create an instance of the object type as follows:

```
objectName = new objectType("value1", "value2")
```

You can create any number of objects by calls to **new**.

DEFINING PROPERTIES

A JavaScript object has properties associated with it. Both the object name and property name are case sensitive.

You define a property by assigning it a value. If you create an object named "myObject," you can give it a property as follows:

```
myObject.color = "Red"
```

An object can have a property that is itself another object.

Access the properties of an object with a simple notation:

```
objectName.propertyName
```

Refer to object properties by full name based on object hierarchy. For example: document.myform.button1.value

INDEXING OBJECT PROPERTIES

In Navigator 2.0, you can refer to an object's properties by their property name or by their ordinal index. In Navigator 3.0 or later, however, if you initially define a property by its name, you must always refer to it by its name; if you initially define a property by an index, you must always refer to it by its index. So if you define object properties initially with an index, such as myObject[5] = "round", you can subsequently refer to the property as myObject[5].

However, this rule does not apply to objects reflected from HTML, such as the forms array. You can always refer objects in these arrays by either their ordinal number (based on where they appear in the document) or their name (if defined). For example, if the second <FORM> tag in a document has a NAME attribute of "myForm", you can refer to the form as document.forms[1] or document.forms["myForm"] or document.myForm.

DEFINING PROPERTIES FOR AN OBJECT TYPE

You can add a property to a previously defined object type by using the prototype property. This defines a property that is shared by all objects of the specified type, rather than by just one instance of the object.

The following code adds a color property to all objects of type car, and then assigns a value to the color property of the object car1.

```
Car.prototype.color=null
car1.color="black"
```

DEFINING METHODS

A **method** is a **function** associated with an **object**.

To define a method, begin by defining the function (*see page 11*). Then use the following syntax to associate the function with an existing object:

```
object.methodname = function_name
```

where object is an existing object, methodname is the name you are assigning to the method, and function_name is the name of the function. Then call the method in the context of the object:

```
object.methodname(params);
```

You can define methods for an object type by including a method definition in the object constructor function. For example,

```
function displayObject() {
   var result = "A Beautiful " + this.color + " " + this.title
   print(result)
}
```

Notice the use of **this** (*see page 42*) to refer to the object to which the method belongs. Make this function a method of myObject by adding the statement

```
this.displayObject = displayObject;
```

to the object definition. So, the full definition of myObject would now look like:

```
function myObject(color, title) {
   this.color = color
   this.title = title
   this.displayObject = displayObject
}
```

Then you can call the displayObject method for each object as:

```
myObject.displayObject()
yourObject.displayObject()
```

CALLING A METHOD

SYNTAX:

```
objectName.methodName(arg1,arg2,arg3...)
```

USING **THIS** FOR OBJECT REFERENCES

JavaScript has a special keyword, **this**, that is used within a method to refer to the current object.

For example, suppose you have a function called validate that validates an object's value property, given the object and the high and low values:

```
function validate(obj, lowval, hival) {
   if ((obj.value < lowval) || (obj.value > hival))
    alert("Invalid Value!")
}
```

Then, you could call validate in each form element'sonChange event handler, using this to pass it the form element, as in the following example:

```
<INPUT TYPE="text" NAME="age" SIZE=3
onChange="validate(this, 18, 99)">
```

In general, **this** refers to the calling object in a method.

When combined with the form property, **this** can refer to the current object's parent form. In the following example, the form myForm contains aText object and a button. When the user clicks the button, the value of theText object is set to the form's name. The button'sonClick event handler uses**this**.form to refer to the parent form, myForm.

```
<FORM NAME="myForm">
Form name:<INPUT TYPE="text" NAME="text1"
VALUE="Beluga">
<P>
<INPUT NAME="button1" TYPE="button"
VALUE="Show Form Name"
   onClick="this.form.text1.value=this.form.name">
</FORM>
```

OBJECT DELETION

In JavaScript for Navigator 2.0, you cannot remove objects — they exist until you leave the page containing the object. In JavaScript for Navigator 3.0, you can remove an object by setting its object reference to null (if that is the last reference to the object). JavaScript finalizes the object immediately, as part of the assignment expression.

CORE OBJECTS

Array An array of elements

CONSTRUCTORS:

new **Array**(*arrayLength*);
new **Array**(*element0, element1, ..., elementN*);

PARAMETERS

arrayLength	(optional): initial length of the array; access this value using length property
elementN	(optional): list of values for the arrays elements; when this form is specified, the array is initialized with the specified values as its elements, and the array's length property is set to the number of arguments

PROPERTIES

index	*read-only*: zero-based index of the match in the string
input	*read-only*: the original string against which the regular expression was matched
length	integer specifying number of elements in an array
prototype	allows the addition of properties to an Array object

METHODS

concat	joins two arrays and returns a new array
join	joins all elements of an array into a string
pop	removes the last element from an array and returns that element
push	adds one or more elements to the end of an array and returns that last element added
reverse	transposes the elements of an array: the first element becomes the last and last becomes first
shift	removes the first element from an array and returns that element
slice	extracts a section of an array and returns a new array

splice	adds and/or removes elements from an array
sort	sorts the elements of an array
toString	returns a string representing the specified object
unshift	adds one or more elements to the front of an array and returns the new length of the array

Boolean An object wrapper for a boolean value

CONSTRUCTOR:

new **Boolean**(*value*)

PARAMETER:

value the initial value of the Boolean object, converted to a Boolean value if necessary; if value is omitted or is 0, null, false, or the empty string (""), the object has an initial value of false; all other values, including the string "false", create an object with an initial value true

PROPERTIES

prototype defines a property that is shared by all Boolean objects

METHODS

toString returns string representing specified object

Date Lets you work with dates and times

CONSTRUCTORS:

new **Date**()

new **Date**("*month day, year hours:minutes:seconds*")

new **Date**(*yr_num, mo_num, day_num*)

new **Date**(*yr_num, mo_num, day_num, hr_num, min_num, sec_num*)

PARAMETERS

month, day, year, hours, minutes, seconds

String values representing part of a date.

yr_num, mo_num, day_num, hr_num, min_num, sec_num Integer values for parts of a date: month is represented by 0 to 11, with 0=January and 11=December.

PROPERTIES

prototype	allows the addition of properties to a date object

METHODS

getDate	returns the day of the month for the specified date
getDay	returns the day of the week for the specified date
getHours	returns the hour in the specified date
getMinutes	returns the minutes in the specified date
getMonth	returns the month in the specified date
getSeconds	returns the seconds in the specified date
getTime	returns the numeric value corresponding to the time for the specified date
getTimezoneOffset	returns the time-zone offset in minutes for the current locale
getYear	returns the year in the specified
date parse	returns the number of milliseconds in a date string since January 1, 1970, 00:00:00, local time
setDate	sets day of the month for a specified date
setHours	sets the hours for a specified date
setMinutes	sets the minutes for a specified date
setMonth	sets the month for a specified date
setSeconds	sets the seconds for a specified date
setTime	sets the value a Date object
setYear	sets the year for a specified date
toGMTString	converts a date to a string, using the Internet GMT conventions
toLocaleString	converts a date to a string, using the current locale's conventions
UTC	returns the number of milliseconds in a Date object since January 1, 1970, 00:00:00, Universal Coordinated Time (GMT)

Function

Specifies a string of JavaScript code to be compiled as a function

CONSTRUCTOR:

new **Function** (*arg1, arg2, ..., argN functionBody*)

PARAMETERS

arg1, arg2, ..., argN (optional) names to be used by the function as formal argument names; each must be a string that corresponds to a valid JavaScript identifier

functionBody a string containing the JavaScript state–ments comprising the function definition

PROPERTIES

arguments	an array corresponding to the arguments passed to the function
arity	indicates the number of arguments expected by the function
caller	specifies which function called the current function
prototype	allows the addition of properties to a Function object

METHOD:

toString	returns a string representing the specified object

Math

Built-in object with properties and methods for mathematical constants and functions

CONSTRUCTOR:

top-level predefined object;
can be accessed without using a constructor or calling method

PROPERTIES

E	Euler's constant and the base of natural logarithms, approximately 2.718
LN10	natural logarithm of 10, approximately 2.302
LN2	natural logarithm of 2, approximately 0.693
LOG10E	base 10 logarithm of E, approximately 0.434

PI	ratio of the circumference of a circle to its diameter, approximately 3.14159
SQRT1 2	square root of 1/2; equivalently, 1 over the square root of 2, approximately 0.707
SQRT2	square root of 2, approximately 1.414

METHODS

abs	returns the absolute value of a number
acos	returns the arccosine (in radians) of a number
asin	returns the arcsine (in radians) of a number
atan	returns the arctangeng (in radians) of a number
atan2	returns the arctangent of the quotient of its arguments
ceil	returns the smallest integer greater than or equal to a number
cos	returns the cosine of a number
exp	returns E^{number}, where *number* is the argument, and *E* is Euler's constant , the base of the natural logarithm
floor	returns the largest integer less than or equal to a number
log	returns the natural logarithm (base E) of a number
max	returns the greater of two numbers
min	returns the lesser of two numbers
pow	returns base to the exponent power, that is, $base^{exponent}$
random	returns a pseudo-random number between 0 and 1
round	returns the value of a number rounded to the nearest integer
sin	returns the sine of a number
sqrt	returns the square root of a number
tan	returns the tangent of a number

Number

Lets you work with numeric values; object wrapper for primitive numeric values

CONSTRUCTOR:

new **Number**(*value*)

PARAMETERS

value	the numeric value of the object being created

PROPERTIES

MAX_VALUE	the largest representable number
MIN_VALUE	the smallest representable number
NaN	special "not a number" value
NEGATIVE_INFINITY	special negative infinite value; returned on overflow
POSITIVE_INFINITY	special infinite value; returned on overflow
prototype	allows the addition of properties to a Number object

METHOD:

toString	returns a string representing the specified object

Object

Primitive JavaScript object type; all objects descend from Object

CONSTRUCTOR:

new Object();

PARAMETERS: none

PROPERTIES

constructor	specifies the function that creates an object's prototype (N3+)
prototype	allows the addition of properties to a Number object

METHODS

eval	evaluates a string of JavaScript code in the context of the specified object (removed as object method in N4, NS3; retained as global function)
toString	returns a string representing the specified object

unwatch	removes a watchpoint from a property of the object (N4, NS3)
valueOf	returns the primitive value of the specified object (N3+)
watch	adds a watchpoint to a property of the object (N4, NS3)

RegExp Contains the pattern of a regular expression; use to find and replace matches in strings

CONSTRUCTOR:

new **RegExp**("*pattern*", "*flags*")
Literal text: /*pattern* /*flags*

PARAMETERS

pattern	the text of the regular expression
flags	(optional) if specified, flags can have one three values: g: global match i: ignore case gi: both global match and ignore case

PROPERTIES

$1, ..., $9	parenthesized substring matches, if any
global	whether or not to test the regular expression against all possible matches in a string, or only against the first
ignoreCase	whether or not to ignore case while attempting to match a string input
($_)	the string against which a regular expression is matched
lastIndex	the index at which to start the next match
lastMatch ($&)	the last matched characters
lastParen ($+)	last parenthesized substring match, if any
leftContext ($`)	the substring preceding the most recent match
multiline ($*)	whether or not to search in strings across multiple lines
rightContext ($')	the substring following the most recent match
source	the text of the pattern

METHODS

compile	compiles a regular expression object
exec	executes a search for a match in its string parameter
test	tests for a match in its string parameter

SPECIAL CHARACTERS IN REGULAR EXPRESSIONS:

\	for characters that are usually treated literally: indicates that the next character is special and not to be interpreted literally; for characters that are usually treated specially: indicates that the next character is not special and should be interpreted literally
^	matches beginning of input or line
$	matches end of input or line
*	matches the preceding character 0 or more times
+	matches the preceding character 1 or more times; equivalent to {1,}
?	matches the preceding character 0 or 1 time
.	matches any single character except the newline character
(x)	matches "x" and remembers the match
x|y	matches either "x" or "y"
{n}	where n is a positive integer, matches exactly n occurrences of the preceding character
{n, }	where n is a positive integer, matches at least n occurrences of the preceding character
{n,m}	where n and m are positive integers, matches at least n and at most m occurences of the preceding character
[xyz]	a character set; matches any one of the enclosed characters; specify a range using a hyphen

[-xyz]	a negated or complemented character set; matches anything not enclosed in the brackets; specify a range of characters using a hyphen
[\b]	matches backspace
\b	matches a word boundary, such as a space
\B	matches a non-word boundary
\cX	where X is a control character, matches a control character in a string
\d	matches a digit character, equivalent to [0-9]
\D	matches any non-digit character; equivalent to [^0-9]
\f	matches a form-feed
\n	matches a linefeed
\r	matches a carriage return
\s	matches a single white space character, including space, tab, form-feed, and linefeed; equivalent to [\f\n\r\t\v]
\t	matches a tab
\v	matches a vertical tab
\w	matches any alphanumeric character including the underscore; equivalent to [A-Za-z0-9_]
\W	matches any non-word character; equivalent to [^A-Zz-z0-9_]
n	where *n* is a positive integer, refers back to the last substring matching the *n* parenthetical in a regular expression (counting left parentheses)
ooctal *xhex*	where *ooctal* is an octal escape value or *xhex* is a hexadecimal escape value; allows you to embed ASCII codes into regular expressions

String — Object representing a series of characters in a string

CONSTRUCTOR:

new **String**(*string*);

PARAMETER:

string	any string

PROPERTIES

length	reflects the length of the string
prototype	allows the addition of properties to a String object

METHODS

anchor	creates an HTML anchor that is used as a hypertext target
big	causes a string to be displayed in a big font as if it were in a <BIG> tag
blink	causes a string to blink as if it were in a <BLINK> tag
bold	causes a string to be displayed as if it were in a <B> tag
charAt	returns the character at the specified index
charCodeAt	retruns a number indicating the ISO-Latin-1 codeset value of the character at the given index
concat	combines the text of two strings and returns a new string
fixed	causes a string to be displayed in a fixed-pitch font as if it were in a <TT> tag
fontcolor	causes a string to be displayed in the specified color as if it were in a <FONT COLOR=color> tag
fontsize	causes a string to be displayed in the specified font size as if it were in a <FONT SIZE=size> tag
fromCharCode	returns a string of numbers that are ISO-Latin-1 codeset values from the specified sequence

indexOf	returns the index of the first occurrence of the specified value within the calling String object
italics	causes a string to be italic, as if it were in an <I> tag
lastIndexOf	returns the index of the last occurrence of the specified value within the calling String object
link	creates an HTML hypertext link that requests another URL
match	used to match a regular expression against a string
replace	used to find a match between a regular expression and a string, and replace the matched substring with a new substring
search	executes the search for a match between a regular expression and a specified string
slice	extracts a section of a string and returns a new string
small	causes a string to be displayed in a small font, as if it were in a <SMALL> tag
split	splits a String object into an array of strings by separating it into substrings
strike	causes a string to be displayed as struck-out text, as if it were in a <STRIKE> tag
sub	causes a string to be displayed as a subscript, as if it were in a <SUB> tag
substr	returns the characters in a string beginning at the specified location through the specified number of characters
substring	returns the characters in a string between two indexes in the string
sup	causes a string to be displayed as superscript, as if it were in a <SUP> tag
toLowerCase	returns the calling string value converted to lowercase
toUpperCase	returns the calling string value converted to uppercase

DOCUMENT OBJECTS

Anchor — A place in a document that is the target of a hypertext link

CONSTRUCTION

<A NAME="anchor_name"> or

theString.**anchor**(*nameAttribute*)

PARAMETERS

theString a String object

nameAttribute a string

PROPERTIES none

METHODS: none

Applet — Includes a Java applet in a web page

CONSTRUCTION

<APPLET CODE="javaCode.class" NAME="applet_name" MYSCRIPT>

PROPERTIES

all public properties of the applet are available for JavaScript access to the Applet object.

METHODS: all public methods of the applet

Area — Defines an area of an image as an image map; Area objects are a type of Link object (*See Link*)

document — Contains information on the current document, and provides methods for displaying HTML output to the user

CONSTRUCTION

HTML <BODY> tag; each Window object has a document property whose value is a document object

EVENT HANDLERS

onClick onDblClick onKeyDown
onKeyPress onKeyUp onMouseDown
onMouseUp

PROPERTIES

alinkColor	a string that specifies the ALINK attribute
anchors	an array containing an entry for each anchor in the document
applets	an array containing an entry for each applet in the document
bgColor	a string that specifies the BGCOLOR attribute
cookie	specifies a cookie
domain	specifies the domain name of the server that served the document
embeds	an array containing an entry for each plug-in in the document
fgColor	a string that specifies the TEXT attribute
formName	a separate property for each named form in the document
forms	an array containing an entry for each form in the document
images	an array containing an entry for each image in the document
lastModified	a string that specifies the date the document was last modified
layers	an array containing an entry for each layer within the document
linkColor	a string that specifies the LINK attribute
links	an array containing an entry for each link in the document
plugins	an array containing an entry for each plug-in in the document
referrer	a string tha specifies the URL of the cqalling document
title	a string that specifies the content of the <TITLE> tag
URL	a string that specifies the complete URL of a document
vlinkColor	a string that specifies the VLINK attribute

METHODS

captureEvents	sets the document to capture all events of the specified type
close	closes an output stream and forces data to display
getSelection	returns a string containing the text of the current selection
handleEvent	invokes the handler for the specified event
open	opens a stream to collect the output of write or writeln methods
releaseEvents	sets the window or document to release captured events of the specified type, sending the events to objects further along the event hierarchy
routeEvent	passes a captured event along the normal event hierarchy
write	writes one or more HTML expressions to a document in the specified window; the write method takes any number of strings that can be literals or variables. Use the string concatenation operator (+) to create one string from several
writeln	writes on or more HTML expressions to a document in the specified window and follows them with a newline character (carriage return or carriage return and linefeed). Ignored by HTML except with in PRE elements

Image An image on an HTML form

CONSTRUCTION

<IMG SOURCE="URL"
NAME="image_name"javaScriptEventHandler>

or new **Image**(*width, height*)

PARAMETERS

width	(optional) image width in pixels
height	(optional) image height in pixels

EVENT HANDLERS

onAbort	onError	onKeyDown
onKeyPress	onKeyUp	onLoad

To define an event handler for an Image object created with the Image constructor:
imageName.eventHandler =
handlerFunction

PROPERTIES

border	reflects the BORDER attribute; string specifying width of image border in pixels
complete	Boolean value indicating whether the web browser has completed its attempt to load the image
height	reflects the HEIGHT attribute; string specifying height of image border in pixels
hspace	reflects the HSPACE attribute; string specifying a margin between left and right edges of an image and the surrounding text in pixels
lowsrc	reflects the LOWSRC attribute; string specifying the URL of a low-resolution version of an image to be displayed in the document
name	reflects the NAME attribute; string specifying the name of an object
prototype	allows the addition of properties to an Image object
src	reflects the SRC attribute; string specifying the URL of an image to be displayed in the document
vspace	reflects the VSPACE attribute; string specifying a margin between top and bottom edges of an image and the surrounding text in pixels
width	reflects the WIDTH attribute; string specifying width of image border in pixels

METHOD:

handleEvent	invokes the handler for the specified event

Layer

Corresponds to a layer in an HTML page and provides a means for manipulating that layer

Construction

<LAYER ID=layer_identifier> or
<ILAYER> or using cascading style sheet syntax

EVENT HANDLERS

onMouseOver	onMouseOut	
onLoad	onFocus	onBlur

PROPERTIES

above	the layer object above this one in z-order, among all layers in the document or the enclosing window object if this layer is topmost
background	the image to use as the background for the layer's canvas
bgColor	the color to use as a solid background color for the layer's canvas
below	the layer object below this one in z-order, among all layers in the document or null if this layer is at the bottom
clip.bottom	the bottom edge of the clipping rectangle (the part of the layer that is visible)
clip.height	the height of the clipping rectangle (the part of the layer that is visible)
clip.left	the left edge of the clipping rectangle (the part of the layer that is visible)
clip.right	the right edge of the clipping rectangle (the part of the layer that is visible)
clip.top	the top edge of the clipping rectangle (the part of the layer that is visible)
clip.width	the width of the clipping rectangle (the part of the layer that is visible)
document	the layer's associated document
left	the horizontal position of the layer's left edge, in pixels, relative to the origin of its parent layer
name	a string specifying the name assigned to the layer through the ID attribute in the <LAYER> tag

pageX	the horizontal position of the layer in pixels, relative to the page
pageY	the vertical position of the layer in pixels, relative to the page
parentLayer	the layer object that contains this layer, or the enclosing window object if this layer is not nested in another layer
siblingAbove	the layer object above this one in z-order (among all layers that share the same parent layer), or null if the layer has no sibling above
siblingBelow	the layer object below this one in z-order (among all layers that share the same parent layer), or null if the layer is at the bottom
src	a string specifying the URL of the layer's contents
top	the vertical position of the layer's top edge in pixels, relative to the origin of its parent layer
visibility	whether or not the layer is visible
zIndex	relative z-order of this layer with respect to its siblings

METHODS

captureEvents	sets the window or document to capture all events of the specified type
handleEvent	invokes the handler for the specified event
load	changes the source of a layer to the contents of the specified file and simultaneously changes the width at which the layer's HTML contents will be wrapped
moveAbove	stacks this layer abover the layer specified in the argument without changing either layer's horizontal or vertical position
moveBelow	stacks this layer below the specified layer, without changing either layer's horizontal or vertical position
moveBy	changes the layer position by applying the specified deltas, measured in pixels

moveTo	moves the top-left corner of the window to the specified screen coordinates
moveToAbsolute	changes the layer position to the specified pixel coordinates within the page (instead of the containing layer)
releaseEvents	sets the layer to release captured events of the specified type, sending the event to objects further along the event hierarchy
resizeBy	resizes the layer by the specified height and width values in pixels
resizeTo	resizes the layer to have the specified height and width values in pixels
routeEvent	passes a captured event along the normal event hierarchy

Link

A piece of text, an image, or an area of an image identified as a hypertext link

CONSTRUCTION

<A HREF="URL" javaScriptEventHandler> or
<AREA HREF="URL" javaScriptEventHandler>

or *theString*.**link**(*hrefAttribute*)

PARAMETERS

theString	a String object
hrefAttribute	any string that specifies the HREF attribute of the A tag; should be a valid URL (relative or absolute)

PROPERTIES

hash	string beginning with hash mark (#) that specifies an anchor name in the URL
host	string that specifies the host and domain name, or IP address, of a network host
hostname	string that specifies the host:port portion of the URL
href	string that specifies the entire URL
pathname	string that specifies the URL-path portion of the URL

port	string that specifies the communications port that the server uses
protocol	string that specifies the beginning of the URL, including the colon
search	string beginning with a question mark that specifies a query string
target	string that specifies the name of the window that displays the content of a clicked hypertext link
text	a string containing the content of the corresponding <A> tag

METHODS

handleEvent	invokes the handler for the specified event

EVENT HANDLERS

for Area objects

onDblClick	onMouseOut	onMouseOver

for Link objects

onClick	onDblClick	
onKeyPress	onKeyDown	onKeyUp
onMouseDown	onMouseUp	
onMouseOut	onMouseOver	

WINDOW OBJECTS

Frame	A window that can display multiple, independently scrollable frames on a single screen, each with its own distinct URL; every frame is a Window object with all the methods and properties of a Window object

CONSTRUCTION

<FRAMESET> <FRAME>

See Window

History	Contains an array of information on the URLs that the client has visited within a window

CONSTRUCTION

History objects are predefined JavaScript objects accessed through the history property of a Window object

PROPERTIES

current	a string specifying the URL of the current history entry
length	reflects the number of entries in the history list
next	a string specifying the URL of the next history entry
previous	a string specifying the URL of the previous history entry

METHODS

back	loads the previous URL in the history list
forward	loads the next URL in the history list
go	loads a URL from the history list

Location Contains information on the current URL; represents the complete URL associated with a given Window object

CONSTRUCTION

Location objects are predefined JavaScript objects accessed through the location property of a Window object

PROPERTIES

Each property represents a different portion of the URL: protocol//host:port/pathname#hash?search

hash	a string beginning with the hash mark (#) that specifies an anchor name fragment in the URL; applies to HTTP URLs only
host	a string specifying the server name, subdomain, and domain name
hostname	a string containing the full hostname of the server, including the server name, subdomain, domain, and port number
href	a string specifying a complete URL
pathname	a string specifying the URL-path portion of the URL
port	a string specifying the communications port that the server uses for communication
protocol	a string specifying the beginning of the URL, up to and including the first colon
search	a string beginning with a question mark that specifies any query information in the URL; applies to HTTP URLs only; the search string contains variable and value pairs, with each pair separated by an ampersand (&)

METHODS

reload	forces a reload of the window's current document
replace	loads the specified URL over the current history entry

screen Contains properties describing the display screen and colors

CONSTRUCTION

JavaScript runtime engine; you can access its properties automatically

PROPERTIES

availHeight	specifies the height of the screen in pixels, minus permanent or semipermanent user interface features displayed by the operating system
availWidth	specifies the width of the screen in pixels, minus permanent or semipermanent user interface features displayed by the operating system
colorDepth	the bit depth of the color palette, if one is in use; otherwise, the value is derived from screen.
height	display screen height
pixelDepth	display screen color resolution (bits per pixel)
width	display screen width

METHODS none

Window Represents a browser window or frame; this is the top-level object for each document, Location, and History object group

CONSTRUCTION

JavaScript runtime engine creates Window object for each body or frameset tag; it also creates a Window object to represent each frame defined in a <FRAME> tag.

Create additional windows by calling the Window.open method.

EVENT HANDLERS

onBlur *	onDragDrop	onError
onFocus *	onLoad	onMove
onResize	onUnload	

*On some platforms in N3, these event handlers have no effect when placed in a frameset tag

PROPERTIES

closed	specifies whether a window has been closed
defaultStatus	reflects the default message displayed in the window's status bar
document	contains information on the current document, and provides methods for displaying HTML output to the user
frames	an array reflecting all the frames in a window
history	contains information on the URLs that the client has visited within a window
innerHeight	specifies the vertical dimension, in pixels, of the window's content area
innerWidth	specifies the horizontal dimension, in pixels, of the window's content area
length	the number of frames in the window
location	contains information on the current URL.
locationbar	represents the browser window's location bar
menubar	represents the browser window's menu bar
name	a unique name used to refer to this window
opener	specifies the window name of the calling document when a window is opened using the open method
outerHeight	specifies the vertical dimension, in pixels, of the window's outside boundary
outerWidth	Specifies the horizontal dimension, in pixels, of the window's outside boundary
pageXOffset	provides the current x-position, in pixels, of a window's viewed page
pageYOffset	provides the current y-position, in pixels, of a window's viewed page
parent	a synonym for a window or frame whose frameset contains the current frame
personalbar	represents the browser window's personal bar (also called the directories bar)

scrollbars	represents the browser window's scroll bars
self	a synonym for the current window
status	specifies a priority or transient message in the window's status bar
statusbar	represents the browser window's status bar
toolbar	Represents the browser window's tool bar
top	A synonym for the topmost browser window
window	A synonym for the current window

METHODS

alert	displays an Alert dialog box with a message and an OK button
back	undoes the last history step in any frame within the top-level window
blur	removes focus from the specified object
captureEvents	sets the window or document to capture all events of the specified type
clearInterval	cancels a timeout that was set with the setInterval method
clearTimeout	cancels a timeout that was set with the setTimeout method
close	closes the specified window
confirm	displays a Confirm dialog box with the specified message and OK and Cancel buttons
disableExternalCapture	disables external event capturing set by the enableExternalCapture method
enableExternalCapture	allows a window with frames to capture events in pages loaded from different locations (servers)
find	finds the specified text string in the contents of the specified window
focus	gives focus to the specified object
forward	loads the next URL in the history list

handleEvent	invokes the handler for specified event
home	points the browser to the URL specified in preferences as the user's home page
moveBy	moves the window by the specified amounts
moveTo	moves the top-left corner of the window to the specified screen coordinates
open	opens a new web browser window
print	prints the contents of the window or frame
prompt	displays a Prompt dialog box with a message and an input field
releaseEvents	sets the window to release captured events of the specified type, sending the event to objects further along the event hierarchy
resizeBy	resizes an entire window by moving the window's bottom-right corner by the specified amount
resizeTo	resizes an entire window to the specified outer height and width
routeEvent	passes a captured event along the normal event hierarchy
scroll	scrolls a window to a specified coordinate
scrollBy	scrolls the viewing area of a window by the specified amount
scrollTo	scrolls the viewing area of the window to the specified coordinates: the specified point becomes the top-left corner
setInterval	evaluates an expression or calls a function every time a specified number of milliseconds elapses
setTimeout	evaluates an expression or calls a function once after a specified number of milliseconds has elapsed
stop	stops the current download

FORM OBJECTS

Button A place in a document that is the target of a hypertext link

CONSTRUCTION

<A NAME="anchor_name"> or

theString.anchor(*nameAttribute*)

PARAMETERS

theString a String object

nameAttribute a string

PROPERTIES: none

METHODS: none

Checkbox A place in a document that is the target of a hypertext link

CONSTRUCTION

<A NAME="anchor_name"> or

theString.anchor(*nameAttribute*)

PARAMETERS

theString a String object

nameAttribute a string

PROPERTIES: none

METHODS: none

FileUpload A place in a document that is the target of a hypertext link

CONSTRUCTION

<A NAME="anchor_name"> or

theString.anchor(nameAttribute)

PARAMETERS

theString: a String object

nameAttribute: a string

PROPERTIES: none

METHODS: none

Form

Lets users input text and make choices from Form elements such as checkboxes, radio buttons, and selection lists. You can also use a form to post data to a server.

CONSTRUCTION

The HTML <FORM> tag.
The JavaScript runtime engine creates a Form object for each <FORM> tag in the document.

DESCRIPTION

Access FORM objects through the document.forms property and through named properties of that object.

To define a form, use standard HTML syntax with the addition of JavaScript event handlers. If you supply a value for the NAME attribute, you can use that value to index into the forms array. In addition, the associated document object has a named property for each named form.

Each form in a document is a distinct object.
You can refer to a form's elements in your code by using the element's name (from the NAME attribute) or the Form.elements array. The elements array contains an entry for each element (such as a Checkbox, Radio, or Text object) in a form.

If multiple objects on the same form have the same NAME attribute, an array of the given name is created automatically. Each element in the array represents an individual Form object. Elements are indexed in source order starting at 0. For example, if two Text elements and a Textarea element on the same form have their NAME attribute set to "myField", an array with the elements myField[0], myField[1], and myField[2] is created. You must be aware of this situation in your code and know whether "myField" refers to a single element or to an array of elements.

EVENT HANDLERS

onReset onSubmit

PROPERTIES

action	reflects the ACTION attribute
elements	an array reflecting all the elements in a form
encoding	reflects the ENCTYPE attribute
length	reflects the number of elements on a form
method	reflects the METHOD attribute
name	reflects the NAME attribute
target	reflects the TARGET attribute

METHODS

handleEvent	invokes the handler for the specified event
reset	simulates a mouse click on a reset button for the calling form
submit	submits a form

Hidden

A Text object that is suppressed from form display on an HTML form. A Hidden object is used for passing name/value pairs when a form submits.

CONSTRUCTION

The HTML <INPUT> tag, with "hidden" as the value of the TYPE attribute. For a given form, the JavaScript runtime engine creates appropriate Hidden objects and puts these objects in the elements array of the corresponding Form object.

DESCRIPTION

Access a Hidden object by indexing this array. You can index the array either by number or by using the value of the NAME attribute when specified.

A Hidden object is a form element and must be defined within a <FORM> tag.

A Hidden object cannot be seen or modified by an end user, but you can programmatically change the value of the object by changing its value property. You can use Hidden objects for client/server communication.

PROPERTIES

form	specifies the form containing the Hidden object
name	specifies the NAME attribute
type	specifies the TYPE attribute
value	specifies the current value of the Hidden object

Option

A selection list.

CONSTRUCTION

The HTML <OPTION> tag or
The Option object constructor or
new **Option**(*text*, *value*, defaultSelected, selected)

After creating an Option object, you can add it to a selection list using the Select.options array.

PARAMETERS

text	(optional) specifies the text to display in the select list
value	(optional) specifies a value that is returned to the server when the option is selected and the object is submitted
defaultSelected	(optional) specifies whether the option is initially selected (true or false)
selected	(optional) specifies the current selection of the option (true or false)

PROPERTIES

defaultSelected	specifies the initial selection state of the object
selected	specifies the current selection state of the option
text	specifies the text for the option
value	specifies the value that is returned to the server when the option is selected and the form is submitted

Password A text field on an HTML form that conceals its value by displaying asterisks (*) when the user enters text into the field.

CONSTRUCTION

The HTML <INPUT> tag with "password" as the value of the TYPE attribute. For a given form, the JavaScript runtime engine creates appropriate Password objects and puts them in element arrays of the corresponding Form object.

DESCRIPTION

Access a Password object by indexing this array. You can index the array either by number or by the value of the NAME attribute if specified.

EVENT HANDLERS

onBlur onFocus

SECURITY

In Navigator 3.0, if a user interactively modifies the value in a password field, you cannot evaluate it accurately unless data tainting is enabled

PROPERTIES

defaultValue	reflects the VALUE attribute
form	specifies the form containing the Password object
name	reflects the NAME attribute
type	reflects the TYPE attribute
value	reflects the current value of the Password object's field

METHODS

blur	removes focus from the object
focus	gives focus to the object
handleEvent	invokes the handler for the specified event
select	selects the input area of the object

Radio

An individual radio button in a set of radio buttons on an HTML form. The user can use a set of radio buttons to choose one item from a list.

CONSTRUCTION

The HTML <INPUT> tag, with "radio" as the value of the TYPE attribute. All radio buttons in a single group must have the same value for the NAME attribute, allowing them to be accessed together.

For a given form, the JavaScript runtime engine creates an individual Radio object for each radio button in that form. It stores all the Radio objects with the same value for the NAME attribute in a single array. It puts that array in the elements array of the corresponding Form object. If a single form has multiple sets of radio buttons, the elements array has multiple Radio objects.

DESCRIPTION

Access a set of buttons by accessing the Form.elements array (either by number or by using the value of the NAME attribute). To access the individual radio buttons in that set, use the returned object array. For example, if your document has a form called "emp" with a set of radio buttons whose NAME attribute is "dept", you would access the individual buttons as document.emp.dept[0], document.emp.dept[1], and so on.

EVENT HANDLERS

onBlur onClick onFocus

PROPERTIES

checked — lets you programmatically select a radio button (property of the individual button)

defaultChecked — reflects the CHECKED attribute (property of the individual button)

form — specifies the form containing the Radio object (property of the array of buttons)

name — reflects the NAME attribute (property of the array of buttons)

type — reflects the TYPE attribute (property of the array of buttons) (N3)

value — reflects the VALUE attribute (property of the array of buttons)

METHODS

blur	removes focus from the radio button (N3)
click	simulates a mouse-click on the radio button
focus	gives focus to the radio button (N3)
handleEvent	invokes the handler for the specified event (N4)

Reset

A reset button on an HTML form. A reset button resets all elements in a form to their defaults.

CONSTRUCTION

The HTML <INPUT> tag, with "reset" as the value of the TYPE attribute. For a given form, the JavaScript runtime engine creates an appropriate Reset object and puts it in the elements array of the corresponding Form object.

DESCRIPTION

Access a Reset object by indexing this array. Index the array either by number or by using the value of the NAME attribute (if supplied).

EVENT HANDLERS

onBlur (N3) onClick onFocus (N3)

PROPERTIES

form	specifies the form containing the Reset object
name	reflects the NAME attribute
type	reflects the TYPE attribute (N3)
value	reflects the VALUE attribute

METHODS

blur	removes focus from the reset button (N3)
click	simulates a mouse-click on the reset button
focus	gives focus to the reset button (N3)
handleEvent	invokes the handler for the specified event (N4)

Select

A selection list on an HTML form. The user can choose one or more items from a selection list, depending on how the list was created.

CONSTRUCTION

The HTML <SELECT> tag. For a given form, the JavaScript runtime engine creates appropriate Select objects for each selection list and puts these objects in the elements array of the corresponding Form object.

DESCRIPTION

You access a Select object by indexing this array. You can index the array either by number or by using the value of the NAME attribute (if supplied).

The runtime engine also creates Option objects for each <OPTION> tag inside the <SELECT> tag.

EVENT HANDLERS

onBlur onChange onFocus

PROPERTIES

form	specifies the form containing the selection list
length	reflects the number of options in the selection list
name	reflects the NAME attribute
options	reflects the <OPTION> tags
selectedIndex	reflects the index of the selected option (or the first selected option, if multiple options are selected)
type	specifies that the object is represents a selection list and whether it can have one or more selected options (N3)

METHODS

blur	removes focus from the selection list
focus	gives focus to the selection list
handleEvent	invokes the handler for the specified event (N4)

Submit

A submit button on an HTML form. A submit button causes a form to be submitted.

CONSTRUCTION

The HTML <INPUT> tag, with "submit" as the value of the TYPE attribute. For a given form, the JavaScript runtime engine creates an appropriate Submit object and puts it in the elements array of the corresponding Form object.

DESCRIPTION

You access a Submit object by indexing this array. You can index the array either by number or by using the value of the NAME attribute (if supplied).

EVENT HANDLERS

onBlur (N3) onClick onFocus (N3)

SECURITY

Navigator 4.0: Submitting a form to a mailto: or news: URL requires the UniversalSendMail privilege.

PROPERTIES

form	specifies the form containing the Submit object
name	reflects the NAME attribute
type	reflects the TYPE attribute (N3)
value	reflects the VALUE attribute

METHODS

blur	removes focus from submit button (N3)
click	simulates a mouse-click on the submit button
focus	gives focus to the submit button (N3)
handleEvent	invokes the handler for the specified event (N4)

Text

A text input field on an HTML form. The user can enter a word, phrase, or series of numbers in a text field.

CONSTRUCTION

The HTML <INPUT> tag, with "text" as the value of the TYPE attribute. For a given form, the JavaScript runtime engine creates appropriate Text objects and puts these objects in the elements array of the corresponding Form object.

DESCRIPTION

Access a Text object by indexing this array. Index the array either by number or by using the value of the NAME attribute (if supplied).

To define a Text object, use standard HTML syntax with the addition of JavaScript event handlers.

EVENT HANDLERS

onBlur onChange onFocus onSelect

PROPERTIES

defaultValue	reflects the VALUE attribute
form	specifies the form containing the Text object
name	reflects the NAME attribute
type	reflects the TYPE attribute (N3)
value	reflects the current value of the Text object's field

METHODS

blur	removes focus from the object
focus	gives focus to the object
handleEvent	invokes the handler for the specified event (N4)
select	selects the input area of the object

Textarea A multiline input field on an HTML form. The user can use a textarea field to enter words, phrases, or numbers.

CONSTRUCTION

The HTML <TEXTAREA> tag. For a given form, the JavaScript runtime engine creates appropriate Textarea objects and puts these objects in the elements array of the corresponding Form object.

DESCRIPTION

You access a Textarea object by indexing this array. You can index the array either by number or by using the value of the NAME attribute (if supplied).

To define a text area, use standard HTML syntax with the addition of JavaScript event handlers.

EVENT HANDLERS

onBlur	onChange	onFocus	onKeyDown
onKeyPress	onKeyUp	onSelect	

PROPERTIES

defaultValue	reflects the VALUE attribute.
form	specifies the form containing the Textarea object
name	reflects the NAME attribute
type	specifies that the object is a Textarea object (N3)
value	reflects the current value of the Textarea object.

METHODS

blur	removes focus from the object
focus	gives focus to the object
handleEvent	invokes the handler for the specified event (N4)
select	selects the input area of the object

BROWSER OBJECTS

MimeType A MIME type (Multipart Internet Mail Extension) supported by the client.

CONSTRUCTION

You do not create MimeType objects yourself. These objects are predefined JavaScript objects that you access through the mimeTypes array of the navigator or Plugin object:

navigator.mimeTypes[index]

where index is either an integer representing a MIME type supported by the client or a string containing the type of a MimeType object (from the MimeType.type property).

DESCRIPTION

Each MimeType object is an element in a mimeTypes array. The mimeTypes array is a property of both navigator and Plugin objects. For example, the following table summarizes the values for displaying JPEG images:

Expression	Value
navigator.mimeTypes["image/jpeg"].type	image/jpeg
navigator.mimeTypes["image/jpeg"].description	JPEG Image
navigator.mimeTypes["image/jpeg"].suffixes	jpeg, jpg, jpe, jfif, pjpeg, pjp
navigator.mimeTypes["image/jpeg"].enabledPlugins	null

PROPERTIES

description a description of the MIME type

enabledPlugin reference to the Plugin object configured for the MIME type

suffixes a string listing possible filename extensions for the MIME type, for example "mpeg, mpg, mpe, mpv, vbs, mpegv"

type the name of the MIME type, for example "video/mpeg" or "audio/x-wav"

METHODS: none

navigator Contains information about the version of Navigator in use.

CONSTRUCTION

The JavaScript runtime engine on the client automatically creates the navigator object.

DESCRIPTION

Use the navigator object to determine which version of the Navigator your users have, what MIME types the user's Navigator can handle, and what plug-ins the user has installed. All of the properties of the navigator object are *read-only*.

PROPERTIES

appCodeName	specifies the code name of the browser
appName	specifies the name of the browser
appVersion	specifies version information for the Navigator
language	indicates the translation of the Navigator being used (N4)
mimeTypes	an array of all MIME types supported by the client (N3)
platform	indicates the machine type for which the Navigator was compiled (N4)
plugins	an array of all plug-ins currently installed on the client. (N3)
userAgent	specifies the user-agent header

METHODS

javaEnabled	tests whether Java is enabled (N3)
plugins.refresh	makes newly installed plug-ins available and optionally reloads open documents that contain plug-ins
preference	allows a signed script to get and set certain Navigator preferences (N4)
taintEnabled	specifies whether data tainting is enabled (N3)

Plugin

A plug-in module installed on the client

CONSTRUCTION

Plugin objects are predefined JavaScript objects that you access through the navigator.plugins array.

DESCRIPTION

A Plugin object is a plug-in installed on the client. A plug-in is a software module that the browser can invoke to display specialized types of embedded data within the browser. The user can obtain a list of installed plug-ins by choosing "About Plug-ins" from the Help menu.

Each Plugin object is an element in the plugins array. Each Plugin object has an array containing one element for each MIME type supported by the plug-in. Each element of the array is a MimeType object. For example, the following code displays the type and description properties of the first Plugin object's first MimeType object.

```
myPlugin=navigator.plugins[0]
myMimeType=myPlugin[0]
document.writeln('myMimeType.type is ',
myMimeType.type,"<BR>")
document.writeln('myMimeType.description is ',
myMimeType.description)
```

The output of the preceding code looks like this:

```
myMimeType.type is video/quicktime
myMimeType.description is QuickTime for Windows
```

The Plugin object lets you dynamically determine which plug-ins are installed on the client. You can write scripts to display embedded plug-in data if the appropriate plug-in is installed, or display some alternative information such as images or text if not.

Plug-ins can be platform dependent and configurable, so a Plugin object's array of MimeType objects can vary from platform to platform, and from user to user.

When you use the <EMBED> tag to generate output from a plug-in application, you are not creating a Plugin object. Use the document.embeds array to refer to plug-in instances created with <EMBED> tags. (See the embeds property of the document object on page 55.)

PROPERTY SUMMARY

description	a description of the plug-in
filename	name of the plug-in file on disk
length	number of elements in the plug-in's array of MimeType objects
name	name of the plug-in

EVENTS

An event is an action that occurs (usually as a result of something the user does). In Navigator 4.0 each event has an associated event object. In Navigator 4.0 you can define methods that capture and handle events before they reach their intended targets (usually the object on which the event occurs).

event

The event object contains properties that describe a JavaScript event, and is passed as an argument to an event handler when the event occurs.
Client-side object (N4)

CONSTRUCTION

Event objects are created by Communicator when an event occurs. You do not create them yourself.

DESCRIPTION

In the case of a mouseDown event, for example, the event object contains the type of event (i.e., mouseDown), the x and y position of the cursor at the time of the event, a number representing the mouse button used, and a field containing the modifier keys (Control, Alt, Meta, or Shift) that were depressed at the time of the event. The properties used within the event object vary from one type of event to another. This variation is provided in the descriptions of individual event handlers (beginning on page 86).

SECURITY

Setting any property of this object requires the UniversalBrowserWrite privilege. In addition, getting the data property of the DragDrop event requires the UniversalBrowserRead privilege.

PROPERTIES

Not all of these properties are relevant to each event type. To learn which properties are used by an event, see the reference for the individual event handler (beginning on page 86).

target	string representing the object to which the event was originally sent (all events)
type	string representing the event type (all events)
data	returns an array of strings containing the URLs of the dropped objects. Passed with the DragDrop event
height	represents the height of the window or frame
layerX	number specifying either the object width when passed with the resize event, or the cursor's horizontal position in pixels relative to the layer in which the event occurred; layerX is synonymous with x
layerY	number specifying either the object height when passed with the resize event, or the cursor's vertical position in pixels relative to the layer in which the event occurred; layerY is synonymous with y
modifiers	string specifying the modifier keys associated with a mouse or key event. Modifier key values are: ALT_MASK, CONTROL_MASK, SHIFT_MASK, and META_MASK
pageX	number specifying the cursor's horizontal position in pixels, relative to the page
pageY	number specifying the cursor's vertical position in pixels, relative to the page
screenX	number specifying the cursor's horizontal position in pixels, relative to the screen
screenY	number specifying the cursor's vertical position in pixels, relative to the screen
which	number specifying either the mouse button that was pressed or the ASCII value of a pressed key. For a mouse, 1 is the left button, 2 is the middle button, and 3 is the right button
width	represents the width of the window or frame

EVENT HANDLERS

An event handler is a JavaScript function or series of statements which handles an event.

SYNTAX: <HTML-ELEMENT eventHandler="JavaScript Code">

onAbort

Executes JavaScript code when an Abort event occurs: when the user aborts the loading of an image (for example by clicking a link or clicking the Stop button). (N3)

EVENT HANDLER FOR:

Image

SYNTAX:

onAbort="*handlerText*"

PARAMETERS

handlerText JavaScript code or a call to a JavaScript function

PROPERTIES

type	indicates the type of event
target	indicates the object to which the event was originally sent

onBlur

Executes JavaScript code when a Blur event occurs: when a form element loses focus or when a window or frame loses focus.

EVENT HANDLER FOR:

Button(N3), Checkbox(N3), FileUpload(N3), Frame(N3), Layer, Password(N3), Radio(N3), Reset(N3), Select(N2), Submit(N3), Text(N2), Textarea(N2), Window(N3)

SYNTAX:

onBlur="*handlerText*"

PARAMETERS

handlerText JavaScript code or a call to a JavaScript function

DESCRIPTION

The blur event can result from a call to the Window.blur method or from the user clicking the mouse on another object or window or tabbing with the keyboard.

For windows, frames, and framesets, onBlur specifies JavaScript code to execute when a window loses focus.

A frame's onBlur event handler overrides an onBlur event handler in the <BODY> tag of the document loaded into frame.

NOTE: In Navigator 3.0, on some platforms placing an onBlur event handler in a <FRAMESET> tag has no effect.

PROPERTIES

type	indicates the type of event
target	indicates the object to which the event was originally sent

onChange

Executes JavaScript code when a Change event occurs: when a Select, Text, or Textarea field loses focus and its value has been modified.

EVENT HANDLER FOR:

FileUpload (N3), Select (N2), Text (N2), Textarea (N2)

SYNTAX:

onChange="*handlerText*"

PARAMETERS

handlerText	JavaScript code or a call to a JavaScript function

DESCRIPTION

Use onChange to validate data after it is modified by a user.

PROPERTIES

type	indicates the type of event
target	indicates the object to which the event was originally sent

onClick

Executes JavaScript code when a Click event occurs: when an object on a form is clicked. (A click event is a combination of the MouseDown and MouseUp events).

EVENT HANDLER FOR:

Button, document, Checkbox, Link, Radio, Reset, Submit

Implemented in N2; N3 added the ability to return false to cancel the action associated with a click event

SYNTAX:

onClick="*handlerText*"

PARAMETERS

handlerText JavaScript code or a call to a JavaScript function

PROPERTIES

type indicates the type of event

target indicates the object to which the event was originally sent

layerX, layerY,
pageX, pageY,
screenX, screenY

represent the cursor location at the time the event occurred (when a link is clicked)

which represents the mouse button: 1 for a left-mouse click and 3 for a right-mouse click

modifiers contains the list of modifier keys held down when the event occurred

DESCRIPTION

For checkboxes, links, radio buttons, reset buttons, and submit buttons, onClick can return false to cancel the action normally associated with a click event.

For example, the following code creates a link that displays a confirm dialog box when clicked. If the user clicks the link and then chooses cancel, the page specified by the link is not loaded.

```
<A HREF = "http://www.mySite.com/"
onClick="return confirm('Load Home page?')">
Home</A>
```

If the event handler returns false, the default action of the object is canceled as follows:

Buttons : no default action; nothing is canceled

Radio buttons and checkboxes : nothing is set

Submit buttons: form is not submitted

Reset buttons: form is not reset

NOTE: In Navigator 3.0, returning false for a reset button in an onClick event handler has no effect on some platforms.

onDblClick

Executes JavaScript code when a DblClick event occurs: when the user double-clicks a form element or a link.

EVENT HANDLER FOR :

document, Link (N4)

SYNTAX:

onDblClick="*handlerText*"

PARAMETERS

handlerText JavaScript code or a call to a JavaScript function

NOTE: DblClick is not implemented on the Macintosh.

EVENT PROPERTIES USED:

type indicates the type of event

target indicates the object to which the event was originally sent

layerX, layerY,
pageX, pageY,
screenX, screenY

represent the cursor location at the time the event occurred

which represents the mouse button: 1 for a left-mouse double-click; 3 for a right-mouse double-click

modifiers contains the list of modifier keys held down when the event occurred onDragDrop Executes JavaScript code when a DragDrop event occurs: when the user drops an object onto the browser window, such as dropping a file. (N4)

EVENT HANDLER FOR:

Window

SYNTAX:

onDragDrop="*handlerText*"

PARAMETERS

handlerText	JavaScript code or a call to a JavaScript function

PROPERTIES

type	indicates the type of event
target	indicates the object to which the event was originally sent
data	returns an array of Strings containing the URLs of the dropped objects
modifiers	contains the list of modifier keys held down when the event occurred
screenX, screenY	represent the cursor location at the time the event occurred

SECURITY

Getting the data property of the DragDrop event requires the UniversalBrowserRead privilege.

DESCRIPTION

The DragDrop event occurs whenever a system item (file, shortcut, and so on) is dropped onto the browser window using the native system's drag and drop mechanism. The browser normally attempts to load the item into the browser window. If the event handler for the DragDrop event returns true, the browser loads the item. If the event handler returns false, the drag and drop is canceled.

onError — Executes JavaScript code when an Error event occurs: when the loading of a document or image causes an error. (N3)

EVENT HANDLER FOR: Image, Window

SYNTAX: onError="*handlerText*"

PARAMETERS

handlerText JavaScript code or a call to a JavaScript function

DESCRIPTION

An error event occurs only when a JavaScript syntax or runtime error occurs, not when a browser error occurs. window.onerror applies only to errors that occur in the window containing window.onerror, not in other windows.

onError can be any of the following:

null to suppress all JavaScript error dialogs. Setting window.onerror to null means your users won't see JavaScript errors caused by your own code.

The *name of a function* that handles errors (arguments are *message text, URL*, and *line number* of the offending line). To suppress the standard JavaScript error dialog, the function must return true.

A variable or property that contains null or a valid function reference.

If you write an error-handling function, you have three options for reporting errors:

Trace errors but let the standard JavaScript dialog report them (use an error handling function that returns false or does not return a value)

Report errors yourself and disable the standard error dialog (use an error handling function that returns true)

Turn off all error reporting (set the onError event handler to null)

PROPERTIES

type	indicates the type of event
target	indicates the object to which the event was originally sent

onFocus Executes JavaScript code when a Focus event occurs: when a window, frame, or frameset receives focus or when a form element receives input focus.

EVENT HANDLER FOR:

Button (N3), Checkbox (N3), FileUpload (N3), Frame (N3), Layer (N4), Password (N3), Radio (N3), Reset (N3), Select (N2), Submit (N3), Text (N2), Textarea (N2), Window (N3)

SYNTAX:

onFocus="*handlerText*"

PARAMETERS

handlerText JavaScript code or a call to a JavaScript function

DESCRIPTION

The focus event can result from a focus method or from the user clicking the mouse on an object or window or tabbing with the keyboard.

Selecting within a field results in a select event, not a focus event. onFocus executes JavaScript code when a focus event occurs.

A frame's onFocus event handler overrides an onFocus event handler in the <BODY> tag of the document loaded into frame.

NOTE: placing an alert in an onFocus event handler results in recurrent alerts. When you press OK to dismiss the alert, the underlying window gains focus again and produces another focus event.

NOTE: In Navigator 3.0, placing an onFocus event handler in a <FRAMESET> tag has no effect on some platforms.

PROPERTIES

type	indicates the type of event
target	indicates the object to which the event was originally sent

onKeyDown Executes JavaScript code when a KeyDown event occurs: when the user depresses a key. (N4)

EVENT HANDLER FOR:

document, Image, Link, Textarea

SYNTAX:

onKeyDown="*handlerText*"

PARAMETERS

handlerText JavaScript code or a call to a JavaScript function

DESCRIPTION

A KeyDown event always occurs before a KeyPress event. If onKeyDown returns false, no KeyPress events occur. This prevents KeyPress events occurring due to the user holding down a key.

PROPERTIES

type	indicates the type of event
target	indicates the object to which the event was originally sent
layerX, layerY, pageX, pageY, screenX, screenY	for an event over a window, these represent the cursor location at the time the event occurred; for an event over a form, they represent the position of the form element
which	represents the ASCII value of the key pressed. To get the actual letter, number, or symbol of the pressed key, use the String.fromCharCode method. To set this property when the ASCII value is unknown, use the String.charCodeAt method.
modifiers	contains the list of modifier keys held down when the event occurred

onKeyPress Executes JavaScript code when a KeyPress event occurs: when the user presses or holds down a key.

EVENT HANDLER FOR:

document, Image, Link, Textarea (N4)

SYNTAX:

onKeyPress="*handlerText*"

PARAMETERS

handlerText JavaScript code or a call to a JavaScript function

DESCRIPTION

A KeyPress event occurs immediately after a KeyDown event only if onKeyDown returns something other than false. A KeyPress event repeatedly occurs until the user releases the key. You can cancel individual KeyPress events.

PROPERTIES

type — indicates the type of event

target — indicates the object to which the event was originally sent

layerX, layerY,
pageX, pageY,
screenX, screenY
— for an event over a window, these represent the cursor location at the time the event occurred; for an event over a form, they represent the position of the form element

which — represents the ASCII value of the key pressed. To get the actual letter, number, or symbol of the pressed key, use the String.fromCharCode method. To set this property when the ASCII value is unknown, use the String.charCodeAt method

modifiers — contains the list of modifier keys held down when the event occurred

onKeyUp

Executes JavaScript code when a KeyUp event occurs: when the user releases a key.

EVENT HANDLER FOR:

document, Image, Link, Textarea (N4)

SYNTAX:

onKeyUp="*handlerText*"

PARAMETERS

handlerText	JavaScript code or a call to a JavaScript function

PROPERTIES

type	indicates the type of event
target	indicates the object to which the event was originally sent
layerX, layerY, pageX, pageY, screenX, screenY	for an event over a window, these represent the cursor location at the time the event occurred; for an event over a form, they represent the position of the form element
which	represents the ASCII value of the key pressed. To get the actual letter, number, or symbol of the pressed key, use the String.fromCharCode method. To set this property when the ASCII value is unknown, use the String.charCodeAt method.
modifiers	contains the list of modifier keys held down when the event occurred

onLoad Executes JavaScript code when a Load event occurs: when the browser finishes loading a window or all frames within a <FRAMESET> tag.

EVENT HANDLER FOR:

Image (N3), Layer (N2), Window (N2)

SYNTAX: onLoad="*handlerText*"

PARAMETERS

handlerText JavaScript code or a call to a JavaScript function

DESCRIPTION

Use the onLoad event handler within either the <BODY> or the <FRAMESET> tag. For example, <BODY onLoad="...">.

In a FRAMESET and FRAME relationship, an onLoad event within a frame (placed in the <BODY> tag) occurs before an onLoad event within the FRAMESET (placed in the <FRAMESET> tag).

For images, the onLoad event handler indicates the script to execute when an image is displayed. Do not confuse *displaying* an image with *loading* an image. You can load several images, then display them one by one in the same Image object by setting the object's src property. In this situation, onLoad executes every time an image is displayed, not just when the image is loaded into memory.

If you specify an onLoad event handler for an Image object that displays a looping GIF animation (multi-image GIF), each loop of the animation triggers the onLoad event, and the event handler executes once for each loop.

You can use the onLoad event handler to create a JavaScript animation by repeatedly setting the src property of an Image object. (See Image)

PROPERTIES

type	indicates the type of event
target	indicates the object to which the event was originally sent
width, height	for an event over a window, but not over a layer, these represent the width and height of the window

onMouseDown Executes JavaScript code when a MouseDown event occurs: when the user depresses a mouse button.

EVENT HANDLER FOR:

Button , document , Link (N4)

SYNTAX:

onMouseDown="*handlerText*"

PARAMETERS

handlerText	JavaScript code or a call to a JavaScript function

DESCRIPTION

If onMouseDown returns false, the default action (entering drag mode, entering selection mode, or arming a link) is canceled.

Arming is caused by a mouseDown over a link. When a link is armed it changes color to represent its new state.

PROPERTIES

type	indicates the type of event
target	indicates the object to which the event was originally sent
layerX, layerY, pageX, pageY, screenX, screenY	represent the cursor location at the time the mouseDown event occurred
which	represents the mouse button: 1 for a left-mouse-button down and 3 for a right-mouse-button down
modifiers	contains the list of modifier keys held down when the mouseDown event occurred

onMouseMove Executes JavaScript code when a MouseMove event occurs: when the user moves the cursor. (N4)

EVENT HANDLER FOR: none

Because mouse movement happens so frequently, by default, onMouseMove is not an event of any object. You must explicitly set it to be associated with a particular object.

SYNTAX:

onMouseMove="*handlerText*"

PARAMETERS

handlerText JavaScript code or a call to a JavaScript function

DESCRIPTION

The MouseMove event is sent only when a capture of the event is requested by an object.

PROPERTIES

type indicates the type of event

target indicates the object to which the event was originally sent

layerX, layerY,
pageX, pageY,
screenX, screenY

represent the cursor location at the time the MouseMove event occurred

onMouseOut Executes JavaScript code when a MouseOut event occurs: each time the mouse pointer leaves an area (client-side image map) or link from inside that area or link. (N3)

EVENT HANDLER FOR:

Layer, Link

SYNTAX:

onMouseOut="*handlerText*"

PARAMETERS

handlerText JavaScript code or a call to a JavaScript function

DESCRIPTION

If the mouse moves from one area into another in a client-side image map, you'll get onMouseOut for the first area, then onMouseOver for the second.

Area objects that use the onMouseOut event handler must include the HREF attribute within the <AREA> tag.

You must return true within the event handler if you want to set the status or defaultStatus properties with onMouseOver.

PROPERTIES

type — indicates the type of event

target — indicates the object to which the event was originally sent

layerX, layerY, pageX, pageY, screenX, screenY — represent the cursor location at the time the MouseOut event occurred

onMouseOver Executes JavaScript code when a MouseOver event occurs: once each time the mouse pointer moves over an object or area from outside that object or area.

EVENT HANDLER FOR:

Area (N3), Layer (N2), Link (N2)

SYNTAX:

onMouseOver="*handlerText*"

PARAMETERS

handlerText JavaScript code or a call to a JavaScript function

DESCRIPTION

If the mouse moves from one area into another in a client-side image map, you'll get onMouseOut for the first area, then onMouseOver for the second.

Area objects that use onMouseOver must include the HREF attribute within the AREA tag.

You must return true within the event handler if you want to set the status or defaultStatus properties with onMouseOver.

PROPERTIES

type indicates the type of event

target indicates the object to which the event was originally sent

layerX, layerY,
pageX, pageY,
screenX, screenY

represent the cursor location at the time the MouseOver event occurred onMouseUp Executes JavaScript code when a MouseUp event occurs: when the user releases a mouse button. (N4)

EVENT HANDLER FOR:

Button, document, Link

SYNTAX:

onMouseUp="*handlerText*"

PARAMETERS

handlerText JavaScript code or a call to a JavaScript function

DESCRIPTION

If onMouseUp returns false, the default action is canceled. For example, if onMouseUp returns false over an armed link, the link is not triggered. Also, if MouseUp occurs over an unarmed link (possibly due to onMouseDown returning false), the link is not triggered.

NOTE: Arming is caused by a MouseDown over a link. When a link is armed it changes color to represent its new state.

PROPERTIES

type indicates the type of event

target indicates the object to which the event was originally sent

layerX, layerY,
pageX, pageY,
screenX, screenY

represent the cursor location at the time the MouseUp event occurred

which represents the mouse button: 1 for a left-mouse-button up and 3 for a right-mouse-button up

modifiers contains the list of modifier keys held down when the MouseUp event occurred

onMove Executes JavaScript code when a Move event occurs: when the user or script moves a window or frame. (N4)

EVENT HANDLER FOR: Window

SYNTAX: onMove="*handlerText*"

PARAMETERS

handlerText JavaScript code or a call to a JavaScript function

PROPERTIES

type indicates the type of event

target indicates the object to which the event was originally sent

screenX, screenY represent the position of the top-left corner of the window or frame

onReset Executes JavaScript code when a Reset event occurs: when a user resets a form (clicks a Reset button). (N3)

EVENT HANDLER FOR: Form

SYNTAX: onReset="*handlerText*"

PARAMETERS

handlerText JavaScript code or a call to a JavaScript function

PROPERTIES

type indicates the type of event

target indicates the object to which the event was originally sent

EXAMPLE:

The following example displays a Text object with the default value "21" and a Reset button. If the user types a state abbreviation in the Text object and then clicks the Reset button, the original value of "21" is restored. The form's onReset event handler displays a message indicating that defaults have been restored.

```
<FORM NAME="myForm" onReset="alert('Defaults have
been restored.')">
State: <INPUT TYPE="text" NAME="age" VALUE="21"
SIZE="3"><P>
<INPUT TYPE="reset" VALUE="Start Over" NAME="reset1">
</FORM>
```

onResize

Executes JavaScript code when a Resize event occurs: when a user or script resizes a window or frame. (N4)

EVENT HANDLER FOR: Window

SYNTAX: onResize="*handlerText*"

PARAMETERS

handlerText JavaScript code or a call to a JavaScript function

PROPERTIES

type indicates the type of event

target indicates the object to which the event was originally sent

width, height represent the width and height of the window or frame

DESCRIPTION

This event is sent after HTML layout completes within the new window inner dimensions. This allows positioned elements and named anchors to have their final sizes and locations queried, image src properties can be restored dynamically, etc.

onSelect

Executes JavaScript code when a Select event occurs: when a user selects some of the text within a Text or Textarea field. (N2)

EVENT HANDLER FOR: Text, Textarea

SYNTAX: onSelect="*handlerText*"

PARAMETERS

handlerText JavaScript code or a call to a JavaScript function

PROPERTIES

type indicates the type of event

target indicates the object to which the event was originally sent

EXAMPLE:

The following example uses onSelect in the "valueField" Text object to call the "selectState" function.

```
<INPUT TYPE="text" VALUE="" NAME="valueField"
onSelect="selectState()">
```

onSubmit Executes JavaScript code when a Submit event occurs: when a user submits a form. (N2)

EVENT HANDLER FOR:

Form

SYNTAX:

onSubmit="*handlerText*"

PARAMETERS

handlerText JavaScript code or a call to a JavaScript function.

SECURITY

Navigator 4.0: Submitting a form to a mailto: or news: URL requires the UniversalSendMail privilege.

DESCRIPTION

You can use onSubmit to prevent a form from being submitted; to do so, put a return statement that returns false in the event handler. Any other returned value lets the form submit. If you omit the **return** statement, the form is submitted.

PROPERTIES

type	indicates the type of event
target	indicates the object to which the event was originally sent

EXAMPLE:

In the following example, onSubmit calls the "validate" function to evaluate the data being submitted. If the data is valid, the form is submitted; otherwise, the form is not submitted.

```
<FORM onSubmit="return validate(this)">
...
</FORM>
```

onUnload Executes JavaScript code when an Unload event occurs: when the user exits a document. (N2)

EVENT HANDLER FOR:

Window

SYNTAX:

onUnload="*handlerText*"

PARAMETERS

handlerText JavaScript code or a call to a JavaScript function.

DESCRIPTION

Use onUnload within either the <BODY> or the <FRAMESET> tag.

For example, <BODY onUnload="..."> .

In a frameset and frame relationship, an onUnload event within a frame (placed in the <BODY> tag) occurs before an onUnload event within the frameset (placed in the <FRAMESET> tag).

PROPERTIES

type	indicates the type of event
target	indicates the object to which the event was originally sent

EXAMPLE:

In the following example, onUnload calls a function named "cleanUp" to perform some shutdown processing when the user exits a Web page:

```
<BODY onUnload="cleanUp()">
```

LIVEWIRE OBJECTS

blob Provides functionality for displaying and linking to BLOb data.

CONSTRUCTION

You do not create a separate blob object. If you know that the value of a cursor property contains BLOb data, you use the methods below to access that data.

SYNTAX:

```
cursorName.colName.blobImage (format,
altText, align, widthPixels, heightPixels,
borderPixels, ismap)
```

METHODS

blobImage displays BLOb data stored in a database

blobLink displays a link that references BLOb data with a link (to store BLOb data in a database, use the blob function)

PARAMETERS

format the image format: GIF, JPEG, or any other MIME image format.

The acceptable formats are specified in the type=image section of the file $nshome\httpd-80\config\mime.types, where $nshome is the directory in which you installed your server. The client browser must also be able to display the image format

altText (optional) the value of the ALT attribute of the <IMG> tag; this indicates text to display if the client browser does not display images

align (optional) the value of the ALIGN attribute of the <IMG> tag: "left", "right", or any other value supported by the client browser

widthPixels	(optional) the width of the image in pixels
heightPixels	(optional) the height of the image in pixels
borderPixels	(optional) the size of the outline border in pixels if the image is a link
ismap	(optional) if this parameter is true, the <IMG> tag has an ISMAP attribute (the image is a clickable map); otherwise it does not have the attribute
Returns	an HTML <IMG> tag for the specified image type

DESCRIPTION

Use blobImage to create an HTML image tag for a graphic image in a standard format such as GIF or JPEG.

The blobImage method fetches a BLOb from the database, creates a temporary file (in memory) of the specified format, and generates an HTML image tag that refers to the temporary file. The JavaScript runtime engine removes the temporary file after the page is generated and sent to the client.

While creating the page, the runtime engine keeps the binary data that blobImage fetches from the database in active memory, so requests that fetch a large amount of data can exceed dynamic memory on the server. Generally, it is good practice to limit the number of rows retrieved at one time, using blobImage to stay within the server's dynamic memory limits.

connection Represents a single database connection from a pool of connections.

CONSTRUCTION

The DbPool.connection method. You do not call a connection constructor directly. Once you have a Connection object, you use it for your interactions with the database.

DESCRIPTION

You can use the prototype property of the Connection class to add a property to all Connection instances. If you do so, that addition applies to all Connection objects running in all applications on your server, not just in the single application that made the change. This allows you to expand the capabilities of this object for your entire server.

PROPERTIES

prototype allows the addition of properties to a Connection object

METHODS

beginTransaction begins a new SQL transaction

commitTransaction commits the current transaction

connected tests whether the database pool (and hence this connection) is connected to a database

cursor creates a database cursor for the specified SQL SELECT statement

execute performs the specified SQL statement. Use for SQL statements other than queries

majorErrorCode major error code returned by the database server or ODBC

majorErrorMessage major error message returned by database server or ODBC

minorErrorCode secondary error code returned by database vendor library

minorErrorMessage secondary message returned by database vendor library

release	releases the connection back to the database pool
rollbackTransaction	rolls back the current transaction.
SQLTable	displays query results. Creates an HTML table for results of an SQL SELECT statement
storedProc	creates a stored-procedure object and runs the specified stored procedure
toString	returns a string representing the specified object

cursor

A Cursor object represents a database cursor for a specified SQL SELECT statement.

CONSTRUCTION

The cursor method of a Connection object or of the database object. You do not call a Cursor constructor.

DESCRIPTION

A database query is said to return a "cursor". You can think of a *cursor* as a virtual table, with rows and columns specified by the query. A *cursor* also has a notion of a current row, which is essentially a pointer to a row in the virtual table. When you perform operations with a *cursor*, they usually affect the current row.

You can perform the following tasks with the Cursor object:

- Modify data in a database table
- Navigate in a database table
- Customize the display of the virtual table returned by a database query

You can use a Cursor object to customize the display of the virtual table by specifying which columns and rows to display and how to display them. The Cursor object does not automatically display the data returned in the virtual table. To display this data, you must create HTML code.

A pointer indicates the current row in a Cursor. When you create a Cursor, the pointer is initially positioned before the first row of the cursor.

The next method makes the following row in the cursor the current row. If the SELECT statement which called the cursor method does not return any rows, the method still creates a Cursor object. However, since that object has no rows, the first time you use the next method on the object, it returns "false". Your application should check for this condition.

IMPORTANT: A database cursor does not guarantee the order or positioning of its rows. For example, if you have an updatable cursor and add a row to the cursor, you have no way of knowing where that row appears in the cursor.

When finished with a Cursor object, use the close method to close it and release the memory it uses. If you release a connection that has an open cursor, the runtime engine waits until the cursor is closed before actually releasing the connection.

If you do not explicitly close a cursor with the close method, the JavaScript runtime engine on the server automatically tries to close all open cursors when the associated database or DbPool object goes out of scope. This can tie up system resources unnecessarily. It can also lead to unpredictable results.

You can use the prototype property of the Cursor class to add a property to all Cursor instances. If you do so, that addition applies to all Cursor instances running in all applications on your server, not just in the single application that made the change. This allows you to expand the capabilities of this object for your entire server.

NOTE: Every Sybase table you use with a cursor must have a unique index.

PROPERTIES

cursorColumn	an array of objects corresponding to the columns in a cursor
prototype	allows the addition of properties to a Cursor object

METHODS

close	closes the cursor and frees the allocated memory
columnName	the name of the column in the cursor corresponding to the specified number.
columns	returns the number of columns in the cursor
deleteRow	Deletes the current row in the specified table
insertRow	Inserts a new row in the specified table
next	Moves the current row to the next row in the cursor
updateRow	Updates records in the current row of the specified table in the cursor

database

Lets an application interact with a relational database.

CONSTRUCTION

The JavaScript runtime engine on the server automatically creates the database object. You indicate that you want to use this object by calling its connect method.

DESCRIPTION

The JavaScript runtime engine on the server creates a database object when an application connects to a database server. Each application has only one database object. You can use the database object to interact with the database on the server. Alternatively, you can use the DbPool and Connection objects.

You can use the database object to connect to the database server and perform the following tasks:

Display the results of a query as an HTML table

Execute SQL statements on the database server

Manage transactions

Run stored procedures

Handle errors returned by the target database

The scope of a database connection created with the database object is a single HTML page. That is, as soon as control leaves the HTML page, the runtime engine closes the database connection. You should close all open cursors, stored-procedure objects, and result sets before the end of the page.

If possible, your application should make the database connection on its initial page. This prevents conflicts from multiple client requests trying to manipulate the status of the connections at once.

Internally, JavaScript creates the database object as an instance of the DbBuiltin class. In most circumstances, this is an implementation detail you do not need to be aware of, because you cannot create instances of this class. However, you can use the prototype property of the DbBuiltin class to add a property to the predefined database object. If you do so, that addition applies to the database object when used in all applications on your server, not just in the single application that made the change. This allows you to expand the capabilities of this object for your entire server.

PROPERTIES

prototype — allows the addition of properties to the database object

METHODS

beginTransaction — begins an SQL transaction

commitTransaction — commits the current SQL transaction

connect — connects to a particular configuration of database and user connected — returns true if the database pool (and hence this connection) is connected to a database

cursor — creates a database cursor for the specified SQL SELECT statement

disconnect — disconnects all connections from the database

execute — performs the specified SQL statement

majorErrorCode — major error code returned by the database server or ODBC

majorErrorMessage — major error message returned by the database server or ODBC

minorErrorCode — secondary error code returned by vendor library

minorErrorMessage — secondary message returned by vendor library

rollbackTransaction — rolls back the current SQL transaction

SQLTable — displays query results. Creates an HTML table for results of an SQL SELECT statement

storedProc — creates a stored-procedure object and runs the specified stored procedure (NS3)

storedProcArgs — creates a prototype for a Sybase stored procedure (NS3)

toString — returns a string representing the specified object

EXAMPLE

This example creates a database object and opens a standard connection to the customer database on an Informix server. The name of the server is "blue", the user name is "ADMIN", and the password is "MANAGER".

```
database.connect("INFORMIX", "blue",
"ADMIN", "MANAGER", "inventory")
```

In this example, many clients can connect to the database simultaneously, but they all share the same connection, user name, and password.

dbPool

Represents a pool of connections to a particular database configuration.

CONSTRUCTION

The DbPool constructor.

To connect to a database, you first create a pool of database connections and then access individual connections as needed.

DESCRIPTION

The lifetime of a DbPool object (its scope) varies. Assuming it has been assigned to a variable, a DbPool object can go out of scope at different times:

If the variable is a property of the project object (such as project.engconn), then it remains in scope until the application terminates or until you reassign the property to another value or to null.

If it is a property of the server object (such as server.engconn), it remains in scope until the server goes down or until you reassign the property to another value or to null.

In all other cases, the variable is a property of the request object. In this situation, the variable goes out of scope when control leaves the HTML page or you reassign the property to another value or to null.

It is your responsibility to release all connections and close all cursors, stored procedures, and result sets associated with a DbPool object before that object goes out of scope. Release connections and close the other objects as soon as you are done with them.

If you do not release a connection, it remains bound and is unavailable to the next user until the associated DbPool object goes out of scope.

When you do call release to give up a connection, the runtime engine waits until all associated cursors, stored procedures, and result sets are closed before actually releasing the connection. Therefore, you must close those objects when you are done with them.

You can use the prototype property of the DbPool object to add a property to all DbPool instances. If you do so, that addition applies to all DbPool objects running in all applications on your server, not just in the single application that made the change. This allows you to expand the capabilities of this object for your entire server.

PROPERTIES

prototype	allows the addition of properties to a DbPool object

METHODS

DbPool Connection	creates a pool of database objects and optionally connects the objects to a particular configuration of database and user
connect	connects the pool to a particular configuration of database and user
connected	tests whether the database pool and all of its connections are connected to a database
connection	retrieves an available connection from the pool
disconnect	dsconnects all connections in the pool from the database
majorErrorCode	major error code returned by the database server or ODBC
majorErrorMessage	major error message returned by database server or ODBC. For server errors, this typically corresponds to the server's SQLCODE
minorErrorCode	secondary error code returned by database vendor library
minorErrorMessage	secondary message returned by database vendor library
storedProcArgs	creates a prototype for a Sybase stored procedure
toString	returns a string representing the specified object

Stproc

Represents a call to a database stored procedure.

CONSTRUCTION

The storedProc method of the database object or of a Connection object. You do not call a Stproc constructor.

DESCRIPTION

Use the close method to close a Stproc object and release the memory it uses when you are finished with it. If you release a connection that has an open stored procedure, the runtime engine waits until the stored procedure is closed before actually releasing the connection.

If you do not explicitly close a stored procedure with the close method, the JavaScript runtime engine on the server automatically tries to close all open stored procedures when the associated database or Connection object goes out of scope. This can tie up system resources unnecessarily and lead to unpredictable results.

You can use the prototype property of the Stproc class to add a property to all Stproc instances. If you do so, that addition applies to all Stproc objects running in all applications on your server, not just in the single application that made the change. This allows you to expand the capabilities of this object for your entire server.

PROPERTIES

prototype	allows the addition of properties to a Stproc object

METHODS

close	closes a stored-procedure object
outParamCount	returns the number of output parameters returned by a stored procedure
outParameters	returns the value of the specified output parameter
resultSet	returns a new result set object
returnValue	returns the return value for the stored procedure

Resultset

Represents a virtual table created by executing a stored procedure.

CONSTRUCTION

The resultSet method of a Stproc object. The Resultset object does not have a constructor.

DESCRIPTION

For Sybase, Oracle, ODBC, and DB2 stored procedures, the stored-procedure object has one Resultset object for each SELECT statement executed by the stored procedure. For Informix stored procedures, the stored-procedure object always has one Resultset object.

A result set has a property for each column in the SELECT statement used to generate the result set. For Sybase, Oracle, and ODBC stored procedures, you can refer to these properties by the name of the column in the virtual table. For Informix and DB2 stored procedures, the columns are not named. For these databases, you must use a numeric index to refer to the column.

Resultset objects are not valid indefinitely. In general, once a stored procedure starts, no interactions are allowed between the database client and the database server until the stored procedure has completed. Three specific circumstances cause a result set to be invalid:

1 If you create a result set as part of a transaction, you must finish using the result set during that transaction. Once you either **commit** or **rollback** the transaction, you can't get any more data from a result set, and you can't get any additional result sets. For example, the following code is illegal:

```
database.beginTransaction();
spobj = database.storedProc("getcusts");
resobj = spobj.resultSet();
database.commitTransaction();
/* Illegal! Result set no longer valid! */
col1 = resobj[0];
```

2 You must retrieve Resultset objects before you call a stored procedure object's returnValue or outParameters methods. Once you call either of these methods, you can't get any more data from a result set or any additional result sets.

```
spobj = database.storedProc("getcusts");
resobj = spobj.resultSet();
retval = spobj.returnValue();
/* Illegal! Result set no longer valid! */
col1 = resobj[0];
```

3 Similarly, you must retrieve result set objects before you call the associated Connection object's cursor or SQLTable methods. For example, the following code is illegal:

```
spobj = database.storedProc("getcusts");
cursobj = database.cursor("SELECT *
    FROM ORDERS;");
/* Illegal! The result set is no longer
    available! */
resobj = spobj.resultSet();
col1 = resobj[0];
```

Use the close method to close the Resultset object and release the memory it uses when you are finished with it. If you release a connection that has an open Resultset, the runtime engine waits until the Resultset is closed before actually releasing the connection.

If you do not explicitly close a Resultset with the close method, the JavaScript runtime engine on the server automatically tries to close all open result sets when the associated database or DbPool object goes out of scope. This can tie up system resources unnecessarily and lead to unpredictable results.

You can use the prototype property of the Resultset class to add a property to all Resultset instances. If you do so, that addition applies to all Resultset objects running in all applications on your server, not just in the single application that made the change. This allows you to expand the capabilities of this object for your entire server.

PROPERTIES

prototype	allows the addition of properties to a Resultset object

METHODS

close	closes a Resultset object
columnName	returns the name of a column in the result set
columns	returns the number of columns in the result set
next	moves the current row to the next row in the result set

SESSION MANAGEMENT SERVICE OBJECTS

client

Contains data specific to an individual client. Server-side object. Netscape Server 3.0: added storedProc and storedProcArgs methods.

CONSTRUCTION

The JavaScript runtime engine on the server automatically creates a client object for each client/application pair.

DESCRIPTION

The JavaScript runtime engine on the server constructs a client object for every client/ application pair. A browser client connected to one application has a different client object than the same browser client connected to a different application. The runtime engine constructs a new client object each time a user accesses an application; there can be hundreds or thousands of client objects active at the same time.

You cannot use the client object on your application's initial page. This page is run when the application is started on the server. At this time, there is not a client request, so there is no available client object.

The runtime engine constructs and destroys the client object for each client request. However, at the end of a request, the runtime engine saves the names and values of the client object's properties so that when the same user returns to the application with a subsequent request, the runtime engine can construct a new client object with the saved data. Thus, conceptually you can think of the client object as remaining for the duration of a client's session with the application. There are several different ways to maintain client property values.

All requests by one client use the same client object, as long as those requests occur within the lifetime of that client object. By default, a client object persists until the associated client has been inactive for 10 minutes. You can use the expiration method to change this default lifetime or the destroy method to explicitly destroy the client object.

Use the client object to maintain data that is specific to an individual client. Although many clients can access an application simultaneously, the individual client objects keep their data separate. Each client object can track the progress of an individual client across multiple requests to the same application.

METHODS

destroy	destroys a client object
expiration	specifies the duration of a client object

lock

Provides a way to lock a critical section of code.

CONSTRUCTION

the Lock constructor:

```
Lock();
```

PARAMETERS None.

failure to construct a new Lock object indicates an internal JavaScript error, such as out of memory

METHODS

lock	obtains the lock
isValid	verifies that this Lock object was properly constructed
unlock	releases the lock

project Contains data for an entire application.

CONSTRUCTION

The JavaScript runtime engine on the server automatically creates a project object for each application running on the server.

DESCRIPTION

The JavaScript runtime engine on the server creates a project object when an application starts and destroys the project object when the application or server stops. The typical project object lifetime is days or weeks.

Each client accessing the same application shares the same project object. Use the project object to maintain global data for an entire application. Many clients can access an application simultaneously, and the project object lets these clients share information.

The runtime engine creates a set of project objects for each distinct Netscape HTTPD process running on the server. Because several server HTTPD processes may be running on different port numbers, the runtime engine creates a set of project objects for each process.

You can lock the project object to ensure that different clients do not change its properties simultaneously. When one client locks the project object, other clients must wait before they can lock it.

METHODS

lock	obtains the lock
unlock	releases the lock

request Contains data specific to the current client request.

CONSTRUCTION

The JavaScript runtime engine on the server automatically creates a request object for each client request.

DESCRIPTION

The JavaScript runtime engine on the server creates a request object each time the client makes a request of the server. The runtime engine destroys the request object after the server responds to the request, typically by providing the requested page.

The properties listed below are read-only properties that are initialized automatically when a request object is created. In addition to these predefined properties, you can create custom properties to store application-specific data about the current request.

PROPERTIES

agent	provides name and version information about the client software
imageX	the horizontal position of the mouse pointer when the user clicked the mouse over an image map
imageY	the vertical position of the mouse pointer when the user clicked the mouse over an image map
inputName	represents an input element on an HTML form (There is not a property whose name is "inputName". Rather, each instance of request has properties named after each input element.)
ip	provides the IP address of the client
method	provides the HTTP method associated with the request
protocol	provides the HTTP protocol level supported by the client's software

METHODS None

server

Contains global data for the entire server. Server-side object. LiveWire 1.0

CONSTRUCTION

The JavaScript runtime engine on the server automatically creates a single server object to store information common to all JavaScript applications running on the web server.

DESCRIPTION

The JavaScript runtime engine on the server creates a server object when the server starts and destroys it when the server stops. Every application on a server shares the same server object. Use the server object to maintain global data for the entire server. Many applications can run on a server simultaneously, and the server object lets them share information.

The runtime engine creates a server object for each distinct Netscape HTTPD process running on the server.

The properties listed below are read-only properties that are initialized automatically when a server object is created. These properties provide information about the server process. In addition to these predefined properties, you can create custom properties.

You can lock the server object to ensure that different applications do not change its properties simultaneously. When one application locks the server object, other applications must wait before they can lock it.

PROPERTIES

host	string specifying the server name, subdomain, and domain name
hostname	string containing the full hostname of the server, including the server name, subdomain, domain, and port number
port	string indicating the port number used for the server
protocol	string indicating the communication protocol used by the server

METHODS

lock	obtains the lock
unlock	releases the lock

EXAMPLE

The following example displays the values of the predefined server object properties:

```
<P>server.host = <SERVER>write(server.host);</SERVER>
<BR>server.hostname = <SERVER>write(server.hostname);</SERVER>
<BR>server.protocol = <SERVER>write(server.protocol);</SERVER>
<BR>server.port = <SERVER>write(server.port);</SERVER>
```

The output of this code displays like this:

server.host = www.myWorld.com

server.hostname = www.myWorld.com:85

server.protocol = http: server.port = 85

UTILITIES

File

Lets an application interact with a physical file on the server. LiveWire 1.0

CONSTRUCTION

the File constructor

new File("*path*")

PARAMETER:

path The path and filename in the format of the server's file system (not a URL path).

DESCRIPTION

Use the File object to write to or read from a file on the server. For security reasons, you cannot programmatically access the file system of client machines.

The File object generates persistent HTML or data files without using a database server. Information stored in a file is preserved when the server goes down.

CAUTION: When using the File object, remember that *an application can read and write files anywhere the operating system allows.* If you create an application that writes to or reads from your file system, you should ensure that users cannot misuse this capability.

When creating a File object, specify the full path, (including the filename) for the path parameter; do *not* use a *relative* path.

If the physical file specified in the path already exists, the JavaScript runtime engine references it when you call methods for the object. If the physical file does not exist, you can create it by calling the open method.

You can display the name and path of a physical file by calling the write function and passing it the name of the related File object.

A pointer indicates the current position in a file. If you open a file in the a or a+ mode, the pointer is initially positioned at the end of the file; otherwise, it is initially positioned at the beginning of the file. In an empty file, the beginning and end of the file are the same. Use the eof, getPosition, and setPosition methods to specify and evaluate the position of the pointer.

You can open a file serveral modes: r[b] opens a file for reading; w[b] opens a file for writing; a[b] opens a file for appending (writing at the end of the file); r+[b] opens a file for reading and writing; w+[b] opens a file for reading and writing; a+[b] opens a file for reading and appending.

You can use the prototype property of the File object to add a property to all File instances. If you do so, that addition applies to all File objects running in all applications on your server, not just in the single application that made the change. This allows you to expand the capabilities of this object for your entire server.

PROPERTIES

prototype	allows the addition of properties to a File object

METHODS

byteToString	converts a number that represents a byte into a string
clearError	clears the current file error status
close	closes an open file on the server
eof	determines whether the pointer is beyond the end of an open file
error	returns the current error status
exists	tests whether a file exists
flush	writes the content of the internal buffer to a file
getLength	returns the length of a file
getPosition	returns the current position of the pointer in an open file
open	opens a file on the server

read	reads data from a file into a string
readByte	reads the next byte from an open file and returns its numeric value
readln	reads the current line from an open file and returns it as a string
setPosition	positions a pointer in an open file
stringToByte	converts the first character of a string into a number that represents a byte
write	writes data from a string to a file on the server
writeByte	writes a byte of data to a binary file on the server
writeln	writes a string and a carriage return to a file on the server

EXAMPLES

Example 1. The following example creates the File object "userInfo" that refers to a physical file called "info.txt" which resides in the same directory as the application's .web file:

```
userInfo = new File("info.txt")
```

Example 2. In the following example, the File object refers to a physical file with an absolute path:

```
userInfo = new File("c:\\data\\info.txt")
```

Example 3. The following example displays the name of a File object onscreen.

```
userInfo = new File("c:\\data\\info.txt")
write(userInfo)
```

SendMail

Sends an email message. Netscape Server 3.0.

CONSTRUCTION

the SendMail constructor:

```
new SendMail();
```

The To and From attributes are required.
All other properties are optional.

PARAMETERS None

DESCRIPTION

Properties specified for the SendMail object are sent in the header of the mail message.

The SendMail object allows you to send either simple text-only mail messages or complex MIME-compliant mail or add attachments to your message. To send a MIME message, set the Content-Type property to the MIME type of the message.

You can use the prototype property of the SendMail object to add a property to all SendMail instances. If you do so, that addition applies to all SendMail objects running in all applications on your server, not just in the single application that made the change. This allows you to expand the capabilities of this object for your entire server.

PROPERTIES

Bcc	comma-delimited list of recipients of the message whose names should not be visible in the message
Body	text of the message
Cc	comma-delimited list of additional recipients of the message
Errorsto	address to which to send errors concerning the message; defaults to the sender's address.
From	user name of the person sending the message
Organization	sender's organization information
prototype	sllows the addition of properties to a SendMail object
Replyto	user name to which replies to the message should be sent; defaults to the sender's address
Smtpserver	mail (SMTP) server name; defaults to the value specified through the setting in the Administration server
Subject	subject of the message
To	comma-delimited list of primary recipients of the message

METHODS

errorCode returns an integer error code associated with sending this message

errorMessage returns a string associated with sending this message

send sends the mail message represented by this object

EXAMPLES:

Example 1: The following script sends mail to abc and xyz, copying jsmith, with the specified subject and body for the message:

```
smMsg = new SendMail();
smMsg.To = "abc@address1.com, xyz@address.com"
smMsg.From = "me@myself.com"
smMsg.Cc = "jsmith@other.com"
smMsg.Subject = "Preamble"
smMsg.Body = "We the people, in order to form a
more perfect union, leap tall buildings in a single
bound, and brush after every meal, do ordain and
establish this constitution."
smMsg.send()
```

Example 2: This example sends an image in a GIF file:

```
sm = new SendMail();
sm.To = "able@baker.com";
sm.From = "cain@citizen.net";
sm.Smtpserver = "pop.mailserver.com";
sm["Errors-to"] = "admin@citizen.net";
sm["Content-type"] = "image/gif";
sm["Content-Transfer-Encoding"] = "base64";
file = new File("/u/cain/LiveWire/mail/picture.gif");
openFlag = file.open("r");
if (openFlag) {
        len = file.getLength();
        str = file.read(len);
        sm.Body = str;
}
sm.send();
```

Example 3: The following example sends a multipart message:

```
sm = new SendMail();
sm.To = "colleague@cmv.msu.edu";
sm.From = "adam@eden.com";
sm.Smtpserver = "mail.server.net";
sm.Organization = "Garden, Inc.";
sm["Content-type"] = "multipart/mixed; boundary=\"-
- - - - - 8B3F7BA67B67C1DDE6C25D04\"";
file = new File("/u/adam/LiveWire/mail/mime");
openFlag = file.open("r");
if (openFlag) {
        len = file.getLength();
        str = file.read(len);
        sm.Body = str;
}
sm.send();
```

The file "mime" has HTML text and an Microsoft Word document separated by the specified boundary. This code sends a message that appears as HTML text followed by the Microsoft Word attachment.

METHODS

Method	*Object*	*Client version*	*Server version*
abs	Math	Nav 2+	LW 1+
acos	Math	Nav 2+	LW 1+
alert	Window	Nav 2+	
anchor	String	Nav 2+	LW 1+
asin	Math	Nav 2+	LW 1+
atan	Math	Nav 2+	LW 1+
atan2	Math	Nav 2+	LW 1+
back	History	Nav 2+	
back	Window	Nav 4	
beginTransaction	Connection		Svr 3
beginTransaction	database		LW 1+
big	String	Nav 2+	LW 1+
blink	String	Nav 2+	LW 1+
blobImage	blob		LW 1+
blobLink	blob		LW 1+
blur	Button	Nav 2+	
blur	Checkbox	Nav 2+	
blur	FileUpload	Nav 2+	
blur	Password	Nav 2+	
blur	Radio	Nav 2+	
blur	Reset	Nav 2+	
blur	Select	Nav 2+	
blur	Submit	Nav 2+	
blur	Text	Nav 2+	
blur	Textarea	Nav 2+	
blur	Window	Nav 3+	
bold	String	Nav 2+	LW 1+
byteToString	File		LW 1+
captureEvents	document	Nav 4	

Method	*Object*	*Client version*	*Server version*
captureEvents	Layer	Nav 4	
captureEvents	Window	Nav 4	
ceil	Math	Nav 2+	LW 1+
charAt	String	Nav 2+	LW 1+
charCodeAt	String	Nav 4	Svr 3
clearError	File		LW 1+
clearInterval	Window	Nav 4	
clearTimeout	Window	Nav 2+	
click	Button	Nav 2+	
click	Checkbox	Nav 2+	
click	Radio	Nav 2+	
click	Reset	Nav 2+	
click	Submit	Nav 2+	
close	Cursor		LW 1+
close	document	Nav 2+	
close	File		LW 1+
close	Resultset		Svr 3
close	Stproc		Svr 3
close	Window	Nav 2+	
columnName	Cursor		LW 1+
columnName	Resultset		Svr 3
columns	Cursor		LW 1+
columns	Resultset		Svr 3
commitTransaction	Connection		Svr 3
commitTransaction	database		LW 1+
compile	RegExp	Nav 4	Svr 3
concat	Array	Nav 4	Svr 3
concat	String	Nav 4	Svr 3
confirm	Window	Nav 2+	
connect	database		LW 1+
connect	DbPool		Svr 3

Method	*Object*	*Client version*	*Server version*
connected	Connection		Svr 3
connected	database		LW 1+
connected	DbPool		Svr 3
connection	DbPool		Svr 3
cos	Math	Nav 2+	LW 1+
cursor	Connection		Svr 3
cursor	database		LW 1+
DbPool	DbPool		Svr 3
deleteRow	Cursor		LW 1+
destroy	client		LW 1+
disableExternalCapture	Window	Nav 4	
disconnect	database		LW 1+
disconnect	DbPool		Svr 3
enableExternalCapture	Window	Nav 4	
eof	File		LW 1+
error	File		LW 1+
errorCode	SendMail		Svr 3
errorMessage	SendMail		Svr 3
eval	Object	Nav 3	LW 1+
exec	RegExp	Nav 4	Svr 3
execute	Connection		Svr 3
execute	database		LW 1+
exists	File		LW 1+
exp	Math	Nav 2+	LW 1+
expiration	client		LW 1+
find	Window	Nav 4	
fixed	String	Nav 2+	LW 1+
floor	Math	Nav 2+	LW 1+
flush	File		LW 1+
focus	Button	Nav 2+	
focus	Checkbox	Nav 2+	

Method	*Object*	*Client version*	*Server version*
focus	FileUpload	Nav 2+	
focus	Password	Nav 2+	
focus	Radio	Nav 2+	
focus	Reset	Nav 2+	
focus	Select	Nav 2+	
focus	Submit	Nav 2+	
focus	Text	Nav 2+	
focus	Textarea	Nav 2+	
focus	Window	Nav 3+	
fontcolor	String	Nav 2+	LW 1+
fontsize	String	Nav 2+	LW 1+
forward	History	Nav 2+	
forward	Window	Nav 4	
fromCharCode	String	Nav 4	Svr 3
getDate	Date	Nav 2+	LW 1+
getDay	Date	Nav 2+	LW 1+
getHours	Date	Nav 2+	LW 1+
getLength	File		LW 1+
getMinutes	Date	Nav 2+	LW 1+
getMonth	Date	Nav 2+	LW 1+
getPosition	File		LW 1+
getSeconds	Date	Nav 2+	LW 1+
getSelection	document	Nav 4	
getTime	Date	Nav 2+	LW 1+
getTimezoneOffset	Date	Nav 2+	LW 1+
getYear	Date	Nav 2+	LW 1+
go	History	Nav 2+	
handleEvent	Button	Nav 4	
handleEvent	Checkbox	Nav 4	
handleEvent	document	Nav 4	
handleEvent	FileUpload	Nav 4	

Method	*Object*	*Client version*	*Server version*
handleEvent	Form	Nav 4	
handleEvent	Image	Nav 4	
handleEvent	Layer	Nav 4	
handleEvent	Link	Nav 4	
handleEvent	Password	Nav 4	
handleEvent	Radio	Nav 4	
handleEvent	Reset	Nav 4	
handleEvent	Select	Nav 4	
handleEvent	Submit	Nav 4	
handleEvent	Text	Nav 4	
handleEvent	Textarea	Nav 4	
handleEvent	Window	Nav 4	
home	Window	Nav 4	
indexOf	String	Nav 2+	LW 1+
insertRow	Cursor		LW 1+
isValid	Lock		Svr 3
italics	String	Nav 2+	LW 1+
javaEnabled	navigator	Nav 3+	
join	Array	Nav 3+	LW 1+
lastIndexOf	String	Nav 2+	LW 1+
link	String	Nav 2+	LW 1+
load	Layer	Nav 4	
lock	Lock		Svr 3
lock	project		LW 1+
lock	server		LW 1+
log	Math	Nav 2+	LW 1+
majorErrorCode	Connection		Svr 3
majorErrorCode	database		LW 1+
majorErrorCode	DbPool		Svr 3
majorErrorMessage	Connection		Svr 3
majorErrorMessage	database		LW 1+
majorErrorMessage	DbPool		Svr 3

Method	*Object*	*Client version*	*Server version*
match	String	Nav 4	Svr 3
max	Math	Nav 2+	LW 1+
min	Math	Nav 2+	LW 1+
minorErrorCode	Connection		Svr 3
minorErrorCode	database		LW 1+
minorErrorCode	DbPool		Svr 3
minorErrorMessage	Connection		Svr 3
minorErrorMessage	database		LW 1+
minorErrorMessage	DbPool		Svr 3
moveAbove	Layer	Nav 4	
moveBelow	Layer	Nav 4	
moveBy	Layer	Nav 4	
moveBy	Window	Nav 4	
moveTo	Layer	Nav 4	
moveTo	Window	Nav 4	
moveToAbsolute	Layer	Nav 4	
next	Cursor		LW 1+
next	Resultset		Svr 3
open	document	Nav 2+	
open	File		LW 1+
open	Window	Nav 2+	
outParamCount	Stproc		Svr 3
outParameters	Stproc		Svr 3
parse	Date	Nav 2+	LW 1+
plugins.refresh	navigator	Nav 3+	
pop	Array	Nav 4	Svr 3
pow	Math	Nav 2+	LW 1+
preference	navigator	Nav 4	
print	Window	Nav 4	
prompt	Window	Nav 2+	
push	Array	Nav 4	Svr 3
random	Math	Nav 2+	LW 1+

Method	*Object*	*Client version*	*Server version*
read	File		LW 1+
readByte	File		LW 1+
readln	File		LW 1+
refresh	navigator.plugins		Nav 3+
release	Connection		Svr 3
releaseEvents	document	Nav 4	
releaseEvents	Layer	Nav 4	
releaseEvents	Window	Nav 4	
reload	Location	Nav 3+	
replace	Location	Nav 3+	
replace	String	Nav 4	Svr 3
reset	Form	Nav 3+	
resizeBy	Layer	Nav 4	
resizeBy	Window	Nav 4	
resizeTo	Layer	Nav 4	
resizeTo	Window	Nav 4	
resultSet	Stproc		Svr 3
returnValue	Stproc		Svr 3
reverse	Array	Nav 3+	LW 1+
rollbackTransaction	Connection		Svr 3
rollbackTransaction	database		LW 1+
round	Math	Nav 2+	LW 1+
routeEvent	document	Nav 4	
routeEvent	Layer	Nav 4	
routeEvent	Window	Nav 4	
scroll	Window	Nav 2-3	
scrollBy	Window	Nav 4	
scrollTo	Window	Nav 4	
search	String	Nav 4	Svr 3
select	FileUpload	Nav 2+	
select	Password	Nav 2+	

Method	*Object*	*Client version*	*Server version*
select	Text	Nav 2+	
select	Textarea	Nav 2+	
send	SendMail	Svr 3	
setDate	Date	Nav 2+	LW 1+
setHours	Date	Nav 2+	LW 1+
setInterval	Window	Nav 4	
setMinutes	Date	Nav 2+	LW 1+
setMonth	Date	Nav 2+	LW 1+
setPosition	File		LW 1+
setSeconds	Date	Nav 2+	LW 1+
setTime	Date	Nav 2+	LW 1+
setTimeout	Window	Nav 2+	
setYear	Date	Nav 2+	LW 1+
shift	Array	Nav 4	Svr 3
sin	Math	Nav 2+	LW 1+
slice	Array	Nav 4	Svr 3
slice	String	Nav 4	Svr 3
small	String	Nav 2+	LW 1+
sort	Array	Nav 3+	LW 1+
splice	Array	Nav 4	Svr 3
split	String	Nav 3+	LW 1+
SQLTable	Connection		Svr 3
SQLTable	database		LW 1+
sqrt	Math	Nav 2+	LW 1+
stop	Window	Nav 4	
storedProc	Connection		Svr 3
storedProc	database		Svr 3
storedProcArgs	database		Svr 3
storedProcArgs	DbPool		Svr 3
strike	String	Nav 2+	LW 1+
stringToByte	File		LW 1+
sub	String	Nav 2+	LW 1+

Method	*Object*	*Client version*	*Server version*
submit	Form	Nav 2+	
substr	String	Nav 4	Svr 3
substring	String	Nav 2+	LW 1+
sup	String	Nav 2+	LW 1+
taintEnabled	navigator	Nav 3	LW 1
tan	Math	Nav 2+	LW 1+
test	RegExp	Nav 4	Svr 3
toGMTString	Date	Nav 2+	LW 1+
toLocaleString	Date	Nav 2+	LW 1+
toLowerCase	String	Nav 2+	LW 1+
toString	Array	Nav 3+	LW 1+
toString	Boolean	Nav 3+	LW 1+
toString	Connection		Svr 3
toString	database		LW 1+
toString	DbPool		Svr 3
toString	Number	Nav 3+	LW 1+
toString	Object	Nav 2+	LW 1+
toUpperCase	String	Nav 2+	LW 1+
unlock	Lock		Svr 3
unlock	project		LW 1+
unlock	server		LW 1+
unshift	Array	Nav 4	Svr 3
unwatch	Object	Nav 4	Svr 3
updateRow	Cursor		LW 1+
UTC	Date	Nav 2+	LW 1+
valueOf	Object	Nav 3+	LW 1+
watch	Object	Nav 4	Svr 3
write	document	Nav 2+	
write	File		LW 1+
writeByte	File		LW 1+
writeln	document	Nav 2+	
writeln	File		LW 1+

PROPERTIES

Property	*Object*	*Client*	*Server*
$1, ..., $9	RegExp	Nav 4	Svr 3
$_	RegExp	Nav 4	Svr 3
$*	RegExp	Nav 4	Svr 3
$&	RegExp	Nav 4	Svr 3
$+	RegExp	Nav 4	Svr 3
$`	RegExp	Nav 4	Svr 3
$'	RegExp	Nav 4	Svr 3
above	Layer	Nav 4	
action	Form	Nav 2+	
agent	request		LW 1+
alinkColor	document	Nav 2+	
anchors	document	Nav 2+	
appCodeName	navigator	Nav 2+	
applets	document	Nav 3+	
appName	navigator	Nav 2+	
appVersion	navigator	Nav 2+	
arguments	Function	Nav 3+	LW 1+
arity	Function	Nav 4	LW 1+
background	Layer	Nav 4	
below	Layer	Nav 4	
bgColor	document	Nav 2+	
bgColor	Layer	Nav 4	
border	Image	Nav 3+	
caller	Function	Nav 3+	LW 1+
checked	Checkbox	Nav 2+	
checked	Radio	Nav 2+	
clip.bottom	Layer	Nav 4	
clip.height	Layer	Nav 4	

Property	*Object*	*Client*	*Server*
clip.left	Layer	Nav 4	
clip.right	Layer	Nav 4	
clip.top	Layer	Nav 4	
clip.width	Layer	Nav 4	
closed	Window	Nav 3+	
colorDepth	screen	Nav 4	
complete	Image	Nav 3+	
constructor	Object	Nav 3+	LW 1+
cookie	document	Nav 2+	
current	History	Nav 3+	
cursorColumn	Cursor		LW 1+
data	event	Nav 4	
defaultChecked	Checkbox	Nav 2+	
defaultChecked	Radio	Nav 2+	
defaultStatus	Window	Nav 2+	
defaultSelected	Option	Nav 3+	
defaultValue	Password	Nav 2+	
defaultValue	Text	Nav 2+	
defaultValue	Textarea	Nav 2+	
description	MimeType	Nav 3+	
description	Plugin	Nav 3+	
document	Layer	Nav 4	
document	Window	Nav 2+	
domain	document	Nav 3+	
E	Math	Nav 2+	LW 1+
elements	Form	Nav 2+	
embeds	document	Nav 3+	
enabledPlugin	MimeType	Nav 3+	
encoding	Form	Nav 2+	
fgColor	document	Nav 2+	
filename	Plugin	Nav 3+	

Method	*Object*	*Client version*	*Server version*
form	Button	Nav 2+	
form	Checkbox	Nav 2+	
form	FileUpload	Nav 2+	
form	Hidden	Nav 2+	
form	Password	Nav 2+	
form	Radio	Nav 2+	
form	Reset	Nav 2+	
form	Select	Nav 2+	
form	Submit	Nav 2+	
form	Text	Nav 2+	
form	Textarea	Nav 2+	
formName	document	Nav 3+	
forms	document	Nav 3+	
frames	Window	Nav 2+	
global	RegExp	Nav 4	Svr 3
hash	Link	Nav 2+	
hash	Location	Nav 2+	
height	event	Nav 4	
height	Image	Nav 3+	
height	screen	Nav 4	
history	Window	Nav 2+	
host	Link	Nav 2+	
host	Location	Nav 2+	
host	server		LW 1+
hostname	Link	Nav 2+	
hostname	Location	Nav 2+	
hostname	server		LW 1+
href	Link	Nav 2+	
href	Location	Nav 2+	
hspace	Image	Nav 3+	
ignoreCase	RegExp	Nav 4	Svr 3

Property	*Object*	*Client*	*Server*
images	document	Nav 3+	
imageX	request		LW 1+
imageY	request		LW 1+
index	Array	Nav 4	Svr 3
input	Array	Nav 4	Svr 3
innerHeight	Window	Nav 4	
innerWidth	Window	Nav 4	
input	RegExp	Nav 4	Svr 3
inputName	request		LW 1+
ip	request		LW 1+
language	navigator	Nav 4	
lastIndex	RegExp	Nav 4	Svr 3
lastMatch	RegExp	Nav 4	Svr 3
lastModified	document	Nav 2+	
lastParen	RegExp	Nav 4	Svr 3
layerX	event	Nav 4	
layerY	event	Nav 4	
layers	document	Nav 4	
left	Layer	Nav 4	
leftContext	RegExp	Nav 4	Svr 3
length	Array	Nav 3+	LW 1+
length	Form	Nav 2+	
length	History	Nav 2+	
length	Plugin	Nav 3+	
length	Select	Nav 2+	
length	String	Nav 2+	LW 1+
length	Window	Nav 2+	
linkColor	document	Nav 2+	
links	document	Nav 2+	
location	Window	Nav 2+	
locationbar	Window	Nav 4	

Property	*Object*	*Client*	*Server*
LN10	Math	Nav 2+	LW 1+
LN2	Math	Nav 2+	LW 1+
LOG10E	Math	Nav 2+	LW 1+
LOG2E	Math	Nav 2+	LW 1+
lowsrc	Image	Nav 3+	
MAX_VALUE	Number	Nav 3+	LW 1+
menubar	Window	Nav 4	
method	Form	Nav 2+	
method	request		LW 1+
mimeTypes	navigator	Nav 3+	
modifiers	event	Nav 4	
MIN_VALUE	Number	Nav 3+	LW 1+
multiline	RegExp	Nav 4	Svr 3
name	Button	Nav 2+	
name	Checkbox	Nav 2+	
name	FileUpload	Nav 2+	
name	Form	Nav 2+	
name	Hidden	Nav 2+	
name	Image	Nav 3+	
name	Layer	Nav 4	
name	Password	Nav 2+	
name	Plugin	Nav 3+	
name	Radio	Nav 2+	
name	Reset	Nav 2+	
name	Select	Nav 2+	
name	Submit	Nav 2+	
name	Text	Nav 2+	
name	Textarea	Nav 2+	
name	Window	Nav 2+	
NaN	Number	Nav 3+	LW 1+
NEGATIVE_INFINITY	Number	Nav 3+	LW 1+

Property	*Object*	*Client*	*Server*
next	History	Nav 3+	
opener	Window	Nav 3+	
options	Select	Nav 2+	
outerHeight	Window	Nav 4	
outerWidth	Window	Nav 4	
pageX	event	Nav 4	
pageX	Layer	Nav 4	
pageXOffset	Window	Nav 4	
pageY	event	Nav 4	
pageY	Layer	Nav 4	
pageYOffset	Window	Nav 4	
parent	Window	Nav 2+	
parentLayer	Layer	Nav 4	
pathname	Link	Nav 2+	
pathname	Location	Nav 2+	
personalbar	Window	Nav 4	
PI	Math	Nav 2+	LW 1+
pixelDepth	screen	Nav 4	
platform	navigator	Nav 4	
plugins	document	Nav 3+	
plugins	navigator	Nav 3+	
port	Link	Nav 2+	
port	Location	Nav 2+	
port	server		LW 1+
POSITIVE_INFINITY	Number	Nav 3+	LW 1+
previous	History	Nav 3+	
protocol	Link	Nav 2+	
protocol	Location	Nav 2+	
protocol	request		LW 1+
protocol	server		LW 1+
prototype	Array	Nav 3+	LW 1+

Property	*Object*	*Client*	*Server*
prototype	Boolean	Nav 3+	LW 1+
prototype	Connection		Svr 3
prototype	Cursor	Nav 3+	LW 1+
prototype	database		LW 1+
prototype	Date	Nav 3+	LW 1+
prototype	DbPool		Svr 3
prototype	File		LW 1+
prototype	Function	Nav 3+	LW 1+
prototype	Image	Nav 3+	LW 1+
prototype	Number	Nav 3+	LW 1+
prototype	Object	Nav 3+	LW 1+
prototype	Resultset		Svr 3
prototype	SendMail		Svr 3
prototype	Stproc		Svr 3
prototype	String	Nav 3+	LW 1+
referrer	document	Nav 2+	
rightContext	RegExp	Nav 4	Svr 3
screenX	event	Nav 4	
screenY	event	Nav 4	
scrollbars	Window	Nav 4	
search	Link	Nav 2+	
search	Location	Nav 2+	
selected	Option	Nav 2+	
selectedIndex	Select	Nav 2+	
self	Window	Nav 2+	
siblingAbove	Layer	Nav 4	
siblingBelow	Layer	Nav 4	
source	RegExp	Nav 4	Svr 3
SQRT1_2	Math	Nav 2+	LW 1+
SQRT2	Math	Nav 2+	LW 1+
src	Image	Nav 3+	

Property	*Object*	*Client*	*Server*
src	Layer	Nav 4	
status	Window	Nav 2+	
statusbar	Window	Nav 4	
suffixes	MimeType	Nav 3+	
target	event	Nav 4	
target	Form	Nav 2+	
target	Link	Nav 2+	
text	Option	Nav 2+	
text	Link	Nav 4	
title	document	Nav 2+	
toolbar	Window	Nav 4	
top	Layer	Nav 4	
top	Window	Nav 2+	
type	Button	Nav 3+	
type	Checkbox	Nav 3+	
type	event	Nav 4	
type	FileUpload	Nav 3+	
type	Hidden	Nav 3+	
type	Password	Nav 3+	
type	MimeType	Nav 3+	
type	Radio	Nav 3+	
type	Reset	Nav 3+	
type	Select	Nav 3+	
type	Submit	Nav 3+	
type	Text	Nav 3+	
type	Textarea	Nav 3+	
URL	document	Nav 2+	
userAgent	navigator	Nav 2+	
value	Button	Nav 2+	
value	Checkbox	Nav 2+	
value	FileUpload	Nav 2+	

Property	*Object*	*Client*	*Server*
value	Hidden	Nav 2+	
value	Option	Nav 2+	
value	Password	Nav 2+	
value	Radio	Nav 2+	
value	Reset	Nav 2+	
value	Submit	Nav 2+	
value	Text	Nav 2+	
value	Textarea	Nav 2+	
visibility	Layer	Nav 4	
vlinkColor	document	Nav 2+	
vspace	Image	Nav 3+	
which	event	Nav 4	
width	event	Nav 4	
width	Image	Nav 3+	
width	screen	Nav 4	
window	Window	Nav 2+	
zIndex	Layer	Nav 4	

JAVA PACKAGES FOR LIVECONNECT

The **LiveConnect** facility alows JavaScript to work with Java objects and Java objects to work with JavaScript objects.

LiveConnect provides two Java applet API packages for communicating with JavaScript:

netscape.javascript and netscape.plugin

The netscape.javascript applet API package is available b*oth on the client and on the server* and has the following classes:

netscape.javascript.JSObject

netscape.javascript.JSException

The netscape.plugin applet API package can be used *only on the client.* It has the following class:

netscape.plugin.Plugin

The following sections describe these classes and list their constructors and methods.

netscape.javascript.JSObject

The public final class JSObject extends Object.

java.lang.Object

```
   |
   +— netscape.javascript.JSObject
```

JSObject allows Java to manipulate objects that are defined in JavaScript.

Values passed from Java to JavaScript are converted as follows:

- JSObject is converted to the original JavaScript object.
- Any other Java object is converted to a JavaScript wrapper, which can be used to access methods and fields of the Java object. Converting this wrapper to a string will call the toString method on the original object. Converting to a number will call the floatValue method if possible and fail otherwise. Converting to a boolean will try to call the booleanValue method in the same way.
- Java arrays are wrapped with a JavaScript object that understands array.length and array[index].
- A Java boolean is converted to a JavaScript boolean.
- Java byte, char, short, int, long, float, and double are converted to JavaScript numbers.

Values passed from JavaScript to Java are converted as follows:

- Objects that are wrappers around Java objects are unwrapped.
- Other objects are wrapped with a JSObject.
- Strings, numbers, and booleans are converted to String, Float, and Boolean objects respectively.

This means that all JavaScript values show up as some kind of java.lang.Object in Java. In order to make much use of them, you will have to cast them to the appropriate subclass of Object, as shown in the following examples:

```
(String) window.getMember("name")
(JSObject) window.getMember("document")
```

NOTE If you call a Java method from JavaScript, this conversion happens automatically—you can pass in "int" argument and it works.

METHODS AND STATIC METHODS

The netscape.javascript.JSObject class has the following **methods**:

call
calls a JavaScript method; equivalent to "this.methodName(args[0], args[1], ...)" in JavaScript.

DECLARATION:

public Object call(String methodName, Object args[])

eval
evaluates a JavaScript expression; the expression is a string of JavaScript source code which will be evaluated in the context given by "this".

DECLARATION:

public Object eval(String s)

getMember
retrieves a named member of a JavaScript object; equivalent to "this.name" in JavaScript.

DECLARATION:

public Object getMember(String name)

getSlot
retrieves an indexed member of a JavaScript object; equivalent to "this[index]" in JavaScript.

DECLARATION:

public Object getSlot(int index)

removeMember
removes a named member of a JavaScript object

DECLARATION:

public void removeMember(String name)

setMember
sets a named member of a JavaScript object; equivalent to "this.name = value" in JavaScript.

DECLARATION:

public void setMember(String name, Object value)

setSlot	sets an indexed member of a JavaScript object; equivalent to "this[index] = value" in JavaScript. DECLARATION: public void setSlot(int index, Object value)
toString	Converts a JSObject to a string; overrides: toString in class Object DECLARATION: public String toString()

The netscape.javascript.JSObject class has the following **static method**:

getWindow	Gets a JSObject for the window containing the given applet; available only on the client. DECLARATION: public static JSObject getWindow(Applet applet)

netscape.javascript.JSException

The public class JSException extends Exception.

java.lang.Object

```
    |
    +— java.lang.Throwable
    |
    +— java.lang.Exception
    |
    +— netscape.javascript.JSException
```

JSException is an exception that is thrown when JavaScript code returns an error.

CONSTRUCTOR:

The netscape.javascript.JSException class has the following constructor:

JSException Constructs a JSException. You specify whether the JSException has a detail message and other information.

DECLARATION:

1. public JSException()
2. public JSException(String *s*)
3. public JSException(String *s*,
   String *filename*,
   int *lineno*,
   String *source*,
   int *tokenIndex*)

ARGUMENTS:

s	the detail message
filename	the URL of the file where the error occurred, if possible
lineno	the line number of the file, if possible
source	the string containing the JavaScript code being evaluated
tokenIndex	the index into the source string where the error occurred

DESCRIPTION

A detail message is a string that describes this particular exception. Each form constructs a JSException with different information:

Form 1 of the declaration constructs a JSException without a detail message.

Form 2 of the declaration constructs a JSException with a detail message.

Form 3 of the declaration constructs a JSException with a detail message and all the other information that usually comes with a JavaScript error.

netscape.plugin.Plugin

The public class Plugin extends Object.

```
java.lang.Object
        |
        +— netscape.plugin.Plugin
```

This class represents the Java reflection of a plug-in. Plug-ins that need to have Java methods associated with them should subclass this class and add new (possibly native) methods to it. This allows other Java entities (such as applets and JavaScript code) to manipulate the plug-in.

CONSTRUCTOR:

Plugin — constructs a Plugin

DECLARATION:

public Plugin()

METHODS

destroy — called when the plug-in is destroyed; it is not necessary to call this method directly; the plug-in will still be active at the point this method is called

DECLARATION:

public void destroy()

See also init

getPeer — returns the native NPP objec: the plug-in instance that is the native part of a Java Plugin object; this field is set by the system, but can be read from plug-in native methods by calling:

NPP npp = (NPP)netscape_plugin_Plugin_getPeer(env, thisPlugin);

DECLARATION:

public int getPeer()

getWindow — returns the JavaScript window on which the plug-in is embedded

DECLARATION:

public JSObject getWindow()

init — Called when the plug-in is initialized; it is not necessary to call this method directly

DECLARATION:

public void init()

See also destroy

isActive — Determines whether the Java reflection of a plug-in still refers to an active plug-in; plug-in instances are destroyed whenever the user leaves the page containing the plug-in, causing the plug-in to become inactive

DECLARATION

public boolean isActive()

JavaScript Security

The JavaScript security model has evolved over time:

- The **same origin policy** is the default policy. It dates from Navigator 2.0, with necessary coverage fixes in Navigator 2.01 and Navigator 2.02.
- Navigator 3.0 offered **data tainting** as a means of providing secure access to specific components on a page. Because signed scripts provide greater security than tainting, tainting has been disabled in Communicator 4.x.
- The **signed script policy** is new to Communicator 4.0. It is based upon the new Java security model, called object signing. To make use of the new policy in JavaScript, you must use the new Java security classes and then sign your JavaScript scripts.

This chapter describes these policies and provides information about using the new security features to create signed JavaScript scripts.

SAME ORIGIN POLICY

The Same Origin Policy will not allow a *script loaded from one origin* to get or set some properties of certain browsers and HTML objects when it loads *a document from a different origin* into a window or frame. Communicator defines the origin as the substring of a URL that includes protocol://host where host includes the optional :port component.

The designated properties of the following objects are subject to this origin check:

image	lowsrc, src
layer	src
location	**All** *except* x and y
window	find
document	For *both read and write*: anchors, applets, cookie, domain, elements, embeds, forms, lastModified, length, links, referrer, title, URL, formName (for each named form), reflectedJavaClass (for each Java class reflected into JavaScript using LiveConnect) For *write only*: all other properties

The only exception to this rule allows a script to set the value of document.domain to a suffix of the current domain. When this happens, the shorter domain is used for subsequent origin checks. For example, if a script in a document at http://www.company.com/dir/other.html executes this statement:

```
document.domain = "company.com";
```

After execution of that statement, another document with the following URL would pass the origin check:

http://company.com/dir/page.html.

CHANGES IN COMMUNICATOR 4.X

To tighten security, some changes have been made to when the origin checks apply. These changes may affect older code with regard to forms and file: URLs.

NAMED FORMS

In Navigator 3.0, named forms were not subject to an origin check even though the document.forms array was. In Communicator 4.0, named forms are also subject to an origin check. *This can cause existing code to break.*

Work around the resulting security errors by creating a new variable as a property of the window object and setting the named form as the value of the variable. Access that variable (and hence the form) through the window object.

FILE: URLS

In Navigator 3.0, when you use <SCRIPT SRC="..."> to load a JavaScript file, the URL specified in the SRC attribute could be any URL type (file:, http:, and so on), regardless of the URL type of the file containing the <SCRIPT> tag.

In Communicator 4.0, if you load a document with any URL other than a file: URL, and that document itself contains a <SCRIPT SRC="..."> tag, the internal SRC attribute can't refer to another file: URL. To get the 3.0 behavior in 4.0, users can add the following line to their preferences file:

```
user_pref("javascript.allow.file_src_from_non_file", true);
```

CAUTION: This preference opens a security hole. Do not set this preference to "true" without an overriding reason for accepting that risk.

ORIGIN CHECKS AND LAYERS

A layer can have a different origin than the surrounding document. If a document has one or more layers, JavaScript checks the origins of those layers before they can interact with each other or with the parent document.

ORIGIN CHECKS AND JAVA APPLETS

Your HTML page can contain <APPLET> tags to use Java applets. If an <APPLET> tag has the MAYSCRIPT attribute, that applet can use JavaScript. In this situation, the applet is subject to origin checks when calling JavaScript. For this purpose, the origin of the applet is the URL of the document that contains the <APPLET> tag.

SIGNED SCRIPT POLICY

A signed script requests expanded privileges, gaining access to restricted information. It requests these privileges by using ***LiveConnect*** and the new Java classes referred to as the ***Java Capabilities API***. These classes add facilities to and refine the control provided by the standard ***Java SecurityManager*** class. You can use these classes to exercise fine control over activities beyond the "sandbox" (the Java term for the carefully defined limits within which Java code must otherwise operate).

Access-control decisions involve defining *who* is allowed to do *what*. In this model, a **principal** represents the *who*, a **target** represents the *what*. The privileges associated with a *principal* represent the authorization (or denial of authorization) to access a specific *target*.

NOTE: Because signed scripts provide greater security, data tainting has been disabled in Communicator 4.x.

CREATING SIGNED SCRIPTS

Several kinds of scripts can be signed: *inline scripts* (those that occur within the <SCRIPT> tag), *event handlers*, *JavaScript entities*, and separate *JavaScript files*.

To sign and package JavaScript scripts that are saved in separate files, use the ***Netscape Signing Tool*** directly. Future versions of the tool will also support signing inline scripts. Until this support is available, Netscape provides the ***Page Signer*** tool as an interim solution.

These tools associate *digital signatures* with scripts on an HTML page. A single HTML page can have scripts signed by different principals.

Each digital signature is owned by a particular *principal* (a real-world entity such as *Columbia University* or *John Smith*). The signature is placed in a ***Java Archive*** (**JAR**) file. For inline scripts, event handlers, and JavaScript entities, Page Signer stores only the *signature* and the *identifier* for the script in the JAR file. For *JavaScript files,* however, the *source* is stored in the JAR file as well.

The associated *principal* allows the user to confirm the validity of the certificate used to sign the script. It also allows the user to ensure that the script has not been altered since it was signed. The user then can decide whether to grant privileges based on the validated identity of the certificate owner and validated integrity of the script.

Remember: a user may deny the privileges requested by your script. You should write your scripts to react gracefully to such decisions.

OBJECT-SIGNING TOOLS

The JavaScript security model for signed scripts is based upon the Java security model for signed objects. This chapter assumes that you are already familiar with the basic principles of object signing, using the Java Capabilities API, and creating digital signatures.

Additional information on these subjects as well as the object-signing tools and documentation can be downloaded from Netscape's website: http://developer.netscape.com/docs/manuals/signedobj/zigbert/index.htm

SSL SERVERS AND UNSIGNED SCRIPTS

An ***SSL server*** provides a simpler alternative to signing scripts with the Page Signer tool. Communicator treats all pages served from a secure server (an SSL server) as if they were signed with the public key of that server. You do not have to sign the individual scripts to get this security. This is particularly helpful if you dynamically generate scripts on your server and have them behave as if they were signed.

CODEBASE PRINCIPALS

JavaScript supports codebase principals, just like Java. A **codebase principal** is a principal derived from the origin of the script rather than by verifying a digital signature of a certificate.

Since codebase principals offer weaker security, they are disabled by default in Communicator, and your scripts should not rely on codebase principals being enabled. You may wish to enable codebase principals while developing your scripts, but you should sign them before delivery.

To enable codebase principals, end users must add the appropriate preference to their Communicator preference file. To do this, add the following line to the file:

```
user_pref("signed.applets.codebase_principal_support", true);
```

Even when codebase principals are disabled, Communicator keeps track of codebase principals to use in enforcement of the Same Origin security policy. *Unsigned scripts* have an associated set of principals with a single element: the codebase principal for the page containing the script. *Signed scripts* also have codebase principals as well as the stronger certificate principals.

With codebase principals enabled, when the user accesses the script, a dialog displays similar to the one displayed with signed scripts. This dialog asks the user to grant privileges *based on the URL* and *does not provide author verification.* It advises the user that the script has not been digitally signed and may have been tampered with.

NOTE: If a page includes signed scripts *and* codebase scripts, *and* signed.applets.codebase_principal_support is enabled, all of the scripts on that page are treated as though they are unsigned, and *codebase principals apply.*

SCRIPTS SIGNED BY DIFFERENT PRINCIPALS

JavaScript differs from Java in important ways that relate to security.

Java signs classes and is able to protect internal methods of those classes through the public/private/protected mechanism. Marking a method as protected or private immediately protects it from an attacker. In addition, any class or method marked final in Java cannot be extended and so is protected from an attacker.

JavaScript, on the other hand, has no concept of public and private methods, so there are no internal methods that could be protected by simply signing a class. In addition, all methods can be changed at runtime, so they must be protected at runtime.

In JavaScript you can add new properties to existing objects, or replace existing properties (including methods) at runtime. You cannot do this in Java. Again, protection that is automatic in Java must be handled separately in JavaScript.

While the *signed script security model* for JavaScript is based on the *object-signing model* for Java, these differences in the languages mean that when JavaScript scripts produced by different principals interact, it is much harder to protect the scripts. Because all of the JavaScript code on a single HTML page runs in the same process, different scripts on the same page can change each other's behavior. For example, one script might redefine a function defined by an earlier script on the same page.

To ensure security, the basic assumption of the JavaScript signed script security model is that mixed scripts on an HTML page operate as if they were all signed by the intersection of the principals that signed each script.

For example, assume principals A and B have signed one script, but only principal A signed another script. In this case, a page with both scripts acts as if it were signed by only A.

In another example, if a signed script and an unsigned script are on the same page, both scripts act as if they were unsigned. This occurs because the signed script has both a codebase principal and a certificate principal, whereas the unsigned script has only a codebase principal. The two codebase principals are always the same for scripts from the same page; therefore, the intersection of the principals for the two scripts yields only the codebase principal. This also happens if both scripts are unsigned.

You can use the import and export functions to allow scripts signed by different principals to interact in a secure fashion. (*For information, see "Importing and Exporting Functions" on page 177.*)

CONTAINER CHECKS: WINDOWS AND LAYERS

In order to protect signed scripts from tampering, Communicator 4.0 adds a new set of checks at the container level, where a container is either a window or a layer. To access the properties of a signed container, the script seeking access must be signed by a superset of the principals that signed the container.

These cross-container checks apply to most properties, whether predefined (by Communicator) or user-defined (by HTML content or by script functions and variables). The cross-container checks do not apply to the following properties of window:

closed	height
outerHeight	outerWidth
pageXOffset	pageYOffset
screenX	screenY
secure	width

If all scripts on a page are signed by the same principals, container checks are applied to the window. If some scripts in a layer are signed by different principals, the special container checks apply to the layer.

To determine which containers are associated with which sets of principals, Communicator uses the following method:

Consider each script on the page in order of declaration, treating javascript: URLs as new unsigned scripts.

1. If this is the first script that has been seen on the page, assign this script's principals to be the principals for the window. (If the current script is unsigned, this makes the window's principal a codebase principal.)
2. If the innermost container (the container directly including the script) has defined principals, intersect the current script's principals with the container's principals and assign the result to be the principals for the container. If the two sets of principals are not equal, intersecting the sets reduces the number of principals associated with the container.
3. Otherwise, find the innermost container that has defined principals. (This may be the window itself, if there are no intermediate layers.) If the principals of the current script are the same as the principals of that container, leave the principals as is.
4. Otherwise, assign the current script's principals to be the principals of the container.

As an illustration of this process, assume a page has two scripts (and no layers), with one script signed and the other unsigned. Communicator first sees the signed script, which causes the window object to be associated with two principals: the *certificate principal* (from the signer of the script) and the *codebase principal* (derived from the location of the page containing the script).

When Communicator sees the second (unsigned) script, it compares the principals of that script with the principals of the current container. The unsigned script has only one principal, the codebase principal. Without layers the innermost container is the window itself, which already has principals.

Because the sets of principals differ, they are intersected, yielding a set with one member, the codebase principal. Communicator stores the result on the window object, narrowing its set of principals. Note that all functions that were defined in the signed script are now considered unsigned. Consequently, mixing signed and unsigned scripts on a page without layers results in all scripts being treated as if they were unsigned.

If the unsigned script is in a layer on the page, this results in different behavior: when Communicator sees the unsigned script, its principals are again compared to those of the signed script in the window and the principals are found to be different. However, now that the innermost container (the layer) has no associated principals, the unsigned principals are associated with the innermost container; the outer container (the window) is untouched. In this case, signed scripts continue to operate as signed. However, accesses by the unsigned script in the layer to objects outside the layer are rejected because the layer has insufficient principals. (*See "Isolating an Unsigned Layer within a Signed Container" on page 175 for more information on this case.*)

IDENTIFYING SIGNED SCRIPTS

You can sign inline scripts, event handler scripts, JavaScript files, and JavaScript entities, but you cannot sign javascript: URLs. You must identify the type of script you're signing within the HTML file:

- To sign an inline script, add both an ARCHIVE attribute and an ID attribute to the <SCRIPT> tag for the script you want to sign. If you do not include an ARCHIVE attribute, Communicator uses the ARCHIVE attribute from an earlier script on the same page.
- To sign an event handler, add an ID attribute for the event handler to the tag containing the event handler. The HTML page must also contain a signed inline script preceding the event handler with a <SCRIPT> tag which supplies the ARCHIVE attribute.

- To sign a JavaScript entity, do not do anything special to the entity. Instead, the HTML page must also contain a signed inline script preceding the JavaScript entity. That SCRIPT tag must supply the ARCHIVE and ID attributes.
- To sign an entire JavaScript file, don't add anything special to the file. Instead, the SCRIPT tag for the script that uses that file must contain the ARCHIVE attribute.

(*Once you've written the HTML file, see "Signing Scripts" on page 183 for information on how to sign it.*)

ARCHIVE attribute

All signed scripts (inline script, event handler, JavaScript file, or JavaScript entity) require a <SCRIPT> tag with an ARCHIVE attribute whose value is the name of the JAR file containing the digital signature. For example, to sign a JavaScript file, you could use this tag:

```
<SCRIPT ARCHIVE="myArchive.jar"
SRC="myJavaScript.js"> </SCRIPT>
```

Event handler scripts do not directly specify the ARCHIVE. Instead, the handler must be preceded by a script containing ARCHIVE. For example:

```
<SCRIPT ARCHIVE="myArchive.jar" ID="a">
...
</SCRIPT>

<FORM>
<INPUT TYPE="button" VALUE="OK"
  onClick="alert('A signed script')" ID="b">
</FORM>
```

Unless you use more than one JAR file, you need only specify the file once. Include the ARCHIVE attribute in the first script on the HTML page and the remaining scripts on the page use the same file. For example:

```
<SCRIPT ARCHIVE="myArchive.jar" ID="a">
document.write("This script is signed.");
</SCRIPT>

<SCRIPT ID="b">
document.write("This script is signed too.");
</SCRIPT>
```

ID ATTRIBUTE

Signed inline and event handler scripts require the ID attribute. The value of this attribute is a string that relates the script to its signature in the JAR file. The ID must be unique within a JAR file.

When a tag contains more than one event handler script, you only need one ID. The entire tag is signed as one piece.

In the following example, the first three scripts use the same JAR file. The third script accesses a JavaScript file so it doesn't use the ID tag. The fourth script uses a different JAR file, and its ID of "a" is unique to that file.

```
<HTML>
<SCRIPT ARCHIVE="firstArchive.jar" ID="a">
document.write("This is a signed script.");
</SCRIPT>

<BODY
  onLoad="alert('A signed script using
firstArchive.jar')"
  onLoad="alert('One ID needed for these event
handler scripts')"
  ID="b">
<SCRIPT SRC="myJavaScript.js">
</SCRIPT>
```

```
<LAYER>
<SCRIPT ARCHIVE="secondArchive.jar" ID="a">
document.write("This script uses the
secondArchive.jar file.");
</SCRIPT>
</LAYER>
</BODY>
</HTML>
```

USING EXPANDED PRIVILEGES

Signed scripts, like Java signed objects, use calls to Netscape's ***Java security classes*** to request expanded privileges.

In the simplest case, you add one line of code asking permission to access a particular target representing the resource you want to access. (*See "Targets" on page 171 for more information.*)

For example:

```
netscape.security.PrivilegeManager.enablePrivilege("UniversalSendMail")
```

When the script calls this function, the signature is verified, and if the signature is valid, expanded privileges can be granted. If necessary, a dialog displays information about the application's author, and gives the user the option to grant or deny expanded privileges.

Privileges are granted only in the scope of the requesting function and only after the request has been granted in that function. This scope includes any functions called by the requesting function. When the script leaves the requesting function, privileges no longer apply.

In the following example, function g requests expanded privileges, and only the commands and functions called *after the request and within function g* are granted privileges.

```
<SCRIPT ARCHIVE="ckHistory.jar" ID="a">
function printEnabled(i) {
  if (history[0] == "") {
    document.write(i + ": disabled<BR>");
  } else {
    document.write(i + ": enabled<BR>");
  }
}

function f() {
  printEnabled(1);
}

function g() {
  printEnabled(2);
  netscape.security.PrivilegeManager.enablePrivilege(
    "UniversalBrowserRead");
  printEnabled(3);
  f();
  printEnabled(4);
}

function h() {
  printEnabled(5);
  g();
  printEnabled(6);
}

printEnabled(7);
h();
printEnabled(8);

</SCRIPT>
```

The code produces the following output:

7: disabled

5: disabled

2: disabled

3: enabled

1: enabled

4: enabled

6: disabled

8: disabled

TARGETS

Accessible types of information, called **targets**, are listed below.

Target	Description
UniversalBrowserRead	Allows reading of privileged data from the browser. This allows the script to pass the same origin check for any document.
UniversalBrowserWrite	Allows modification of privileged data in a browser. This allows the script to pass the same origin check for any document.
UniversalBrowserAccess	Allows both reading and modification of privileged data from the browser. This allows the script to pass the same origin check for any document.
UniversalFileRead	Allows a script to read any files stored on hard disks or other storage media connected to your computer.
UniversalPreferencesRead	Allows the script to read preferences using the navigator.preference method.
UniversalPreferencesWrite	Allows the script to set preferences using the navigator.preference method.
UniversalSendMail	Allows the program to send mail in the user's name.

JAVASCRIPT FEATURES REQUIRING PRIVILEGES

This section lists the JavaScript features that require expanded privileges and the target used to access each feature. Unsigned scripts cannot use any of these features, unless the end user has enabled codebase principals.

- Setting a file upload widget requires UniversalFileRead.
- Submitting a form to a mailto: or news: URL requires UniversalSendMail.
- Using an about: URL other than about:blank requires UniversalBrowserRead.
- event object: Setting any property requires UniversalBrowserWrite.
- DragDrop event: Getting the value of the data property requires UniversalBrowserRead.
- history object: Getting the value of any property requires UniversalBrowserRead.
- navigator object:
  Getting the value of a preference using the preference method requires UniversalPreferencesRead.
  Setting the value of a preference using the preference method requires UniversalPreferencesWrite.
- window object:
  Permission for the following operations requires UniversalBrowserWrite.

Adding or removing the directory bar, location bar, menu bar, personal bar, scroll bar, status bar, or toolbar.

Using the methods in the following table under the indicated circumstances

enableExternalCapture	To capture events in pages loaded from different servers. Follow this method with captureEvents.
close	To unconditionally close a browser window.
moveBy	To move a window offscreen.
moveTo	To move a window offscreen.
open	To create a window smaller than 100 x 100 pixels or larger than the screen can accommodate by using innerWidth, innerHeight, outerWidth, and outerHeight. To place a window off screen by using screenX and screenY. To create a window without a titlebar by using titlebar. To use alwaysRaised, alwaysLowered, or z-lock for any setting.
resizeTo	To resize a window smaller than 100 x 100 pixels or larger than the screen can accommodate.
resizeBy	To resize a window smaller than 100 x 100 pixels or larger than the screen can accommodate.

Setting the properties in the following table under the indicated circumstances:

innerWidth	To set the inner width of a window to a size smaller than 100 x 100 or larger than the screen can accommodate.
innerHeight	To set the inner height of a window to a size smaller than 100 x 100 or larger than the screen can accommodate.

Example

The following script includes a button, that displays an alert dialog containing part of the URL history of the browser. To work properly, the script must be signed.

```
<SCRIPT ARCHIVE="myArchive.jar" ID="a">

function getHistory(i) {
  //Attempt to access privileged information
  return history[i];
}

function getImmediateHistory() {
  //Request privilege
  netscape.security.PrivilegeManager.enablePrivilege(
    "UniversalBrowserRead");
  return getHistory(1);
}

</SCRIPT>
...
<INPUT TYPE="button"
onClick="alert(getImmediateHistory());" ID="b">
```

WRITING THE SCRIPT

Here are special considerations for writing signed scripts.

CAPTURING EVENTS FROM OTHER LOCATIONS

If a window with frames needs to capture events in pages loaded from different locations (servers), use the enableExternalCapture method in a signed script requesting UniversalBrowserWrite privileges. Use this method before calling the captureEvents method. For example, with the following code the window can capture all Click events that occur across its frames.

```
<SCRIPT ARCHIVE="myArchive.jar" ID="archive">
...
function captureClicks() {
  netscape.security.PrivilegeManager.enablePrivilege("UniversalBrowserWrite");
  enableExternalCapture();
  captureEvents(Event.CLICK);
  ...
}
...
</SCRIPT>
```

ISOLATING AN UNSIGNED LAYER WITHIN A SIGNED CONTAINER

To create an unsigned layer within a signed container, you need to perform some additional steps to make scripts in the unsigned layer work properly.

- Set the __parent__ property of the layer object to null so that variable lookups performed by the script in the unsigned layer do not follow the parent chain up to the window object and attempt to access the window object's properties, which are protected by the container check.
- Because standard objects (String, Array, Date, and so on) are defined in the window object and not normally in the layer, you must call the initStandardObjects method of the layer object. This creates copies of the standard objects in the layer's scope.

INTERNATIONAL CHARACTERS IN SIGNED SCRIPTS

When used in scripts, international characters can appear in string constants and in comments. JavaScript keywords and variables cannot include special international characters.

Scripts that include international characters cannot be signed because the process of transforming the characters to the local character set invalidates the signature.

To work around this limitation:

- Escape the international characters ('0x\ea', and so on).
- Put the data containing the international characters in a hidden form element, and access the form element through the signed script.
- Separate signed and unsigned scripts into different layers, and use the international characters in the unsigned scripts.
- Remove comments that include international characters.

There is no restriction on international characters the HTML surrounding the signed scripts.

IMPORTING AND EXPORTING FUNCTIONS

You might want to provide interfaces to call into secure containers (windows and layers). To do so, you use the import and export statements. Exporting a function name makes it available to be imported by scripts outside the container without being subject to a container test.

You can only import and export functions, either top-level functions (associated with a window object) or methods of some other object. You cannot import or export entire objects or properties that aren't functions.

Importing a function into your scope creates a new function of the same name as the imported function. Calling that function calls the corresponding function from the secure container.

To use import and export, you must explicitly set the LANGUAGE attribute of the SCRIPT tag to "JavaScript1.2".

In the signed script that defines a function you want to let other scripts access, use the export statement. The syntax of this statement is:

exportStmt ::= export exprList

exprList ::= expr | expr, exprList

where each expr must resolve to the name of a function. The export statement marks each function as importable.

In the script in which you want to import that function, use the import statement. The syntax of this statement is:

importStmt ::= import importList

importList ::= importElem | importElem, importList

importElem ::= expr.funName | expr.*

Executing import expr.funName evaluates expr and then imports the funName function of that object into the current scope. It is an error if expr does not evaluate to an object, if there is no function named "funName", or if the function exists but has not been marked as importable. Executing import expr.* imports all importable functions of expr.

EXAMPLE

The following example has three pages in a frameset. The file containerAccess.html defines the frameset and calls a user function when the frameset is loaded. One page, secureContainer.html, has signed scripts and exports a function. The other page, access.html, imports the exported function and calls it.

While this example exports a function that does not enable or require expanded privileges, you can export functions that do enable privileges. If you do so, you should be very careful to not inadvertently allow access to an attacker.

File: containerAccess.html

```
<HTML>
<FRAMESET NAME=myframes ROWS="50%,*"
onLoad="inner.myOnLoad()">
<FRAME NAME=inner SRC="access.html">
<FRAME NAME=secureContainer
SRC="secureContainer.html">
</FRAMESET>
</HTML>
```

File: secureContainer.html

```
<HTML>
This page defines a variable and two functions.
Only one function, publicFunction, is exported.
<BR>

<SCRIPT ARCHIVE="secureContainer.jar"
LANGUAGE="JavaScript1.2" ID="a">
function privateFunction() {
  return 7;
}
var privateVariable = 23;
function publicFunction() {
  return 34;
}
export publicFunction;
netscape.security.PrivilegeManager.enablePrivilege(
  "UniversalBrowserRead");
document.write("This page is at " + history[0]);
// Privileges revert automatically when the script
terminates.
</SCRIPT>
</HTML>
```

File: access.html

```
<HTML>
This page attempts to access an exported function
from a signed
container. The access should succeed.

<SCRIPT LANGUAGE="JavaScript1.2">

function myOnLoad() {
  var ctnr = top.frames.secureContainer;
  import ctnr.publicFunction;
  alert("value is " + publicFunction());
}

</SCRIPT>
</HTML>
```

HINTS FOR WRITING SECURE JAVASCRIPT

Check the Location of the Script

If you have signed scripts in pages you have posted to your site, it is possible to copy the JAR file from your site and post it on another site. As long as the signed scripts themselves are not altered, the scripts will continue to operate under your signature. (*See "Debugging Invalid Hash Errors" on page 184 for one exception to this rule.*)

If you wish to prevent this, you can force your scripts to work only from your site.

```
<SCRIPT ARCHIVE="siteSpecific.jar" ID="a"
LANGUAGE="JavaScript1.2">
if (document.URL.match(/^http:\/\/
www.company.com\//)) {
  netscape.security.PrivilegeManager.enablePrivilege(...);
  // Do your stuff
}
</SCRIPT>
```

Then if the JAR file and script are copied to another site, they no longer work. If the person who copies the script alters it to bypass the check on the source of the script, the signature is invalidated.

Be Careful What You Export

When you export functions from your signed script, you are in effect transferring any trust the user has placed in you to any script that calls your functions. This means you have a responsibility to ensure that you are not exporting interfaces that can be used in ways you do not want. For example, the following program exports a call to eval that can operate under expanded privileges.

```
<SCRIPT ARCHIVE="duh.jar" ID="a">
function myEval(s) {
  netscape.security.PrivilegeManager.enablePrivilege(
    "UniversalFileAccess");
  return eval(s);
}
export myEval; // Don't do this!!!!
</SCRIPT>
```

Now any other script can import myEval and read and write any file on the user's hard disk using trust the user has granted to you.

Minimize the Trusted Code Base

In security parlance, the **trusted code base** (**TCB**) is the set of code that has privileges to perform restricted actions. One way to improve security is reduce the size of the TCB, which then gives fewer points for attack or opportunities for mistakes.

For example, the following code, if executed in a signed script with the user's approval, opens a new window containing the history of the browser:

```
<SCRIPT ARCHIVE="historyWin.jar" ID="a">
netscape.security.PrivilegeManager.enablePrivilege(
  "UniversalBrowserAccess");
var win = window.open();
for (var i=0; i < history.length; i++) {
  win.document.writeln(history[i] + "<BR>");
}
win.close();
</SCRIPT>
```

The TCB in this instance is the entire script because privileges are acquired at the beginning and never reverted. You could reduce the TCB by rewriting the program as follows:

```
<SCRIPT ARCHIVE="historyWin.jar" ID="a">
var win = window.open();
netscape.security.PrivilegeManager.enablePrivilege(
  "UniversalBrowserAccess");
for (var i=0; i < history.length; i++) {
  win.document.writeln(history[i] + "<BR>");
}
netscape.security.PrivilegeManager.revertPrivilege(
  "UniversalBrowserAccess");
win.close();
</SCRIPT>
```

With this change, the TCB becomes only the loop containing the accesses to the history property. You could avoid the extra call into Java to revert the privilege by introducing a function:

```
<SCRIPT ARCHIVE="historyWin.jar" ID="a">
function writeArray() {
  netscape.security.PrivilegeManager.enablePrivilege(
    "UniversalBrowserAccess");
```

```
  for (var i=0; i < history.length; i++) {
    win.document.writeln(history[i] + "<BR>");
  }
}
var win = window.open();
writeArray();
win.close();
</SCRIPT>
```

The privileges are automatically reverted when writeArray returns, so you don't have to do so explicitly.

Use the Minimal Capability Required for the Task

Another way of reducing your exposure to exploits or mistakes is by using only the minimal capability required to perform the given access. For example, the previous code requested UniversalBrowserAccess, which is a macro target containing both UniversalBrowserRead and UniversalBrowserWrite. Only UniversalBrowserRead is required to read the elements of the history array, so you could rewrite the above code more securely:

```
<SCRIPT ARCHIVE="historyWin.jar" ID="a">
function writeArray() {
  netscape.security.PrivilegeManager.enablePrivilege(
    "UniversalBrowserRead");
  for (var i=0; i < history.length; i++) {
    win.document.writeln(history[i] + "<BR>");
  }
}
var win = window.open();
writeArray();
win.close();
</SCRIPT>
```

SIGNING SCRIPTS

When developing a script that you intend to sign, you can use codebase principals for testing, as described in "Codebase Principals" on page 162. After modifying the script, you must to sign it.

For any script to be granted expanded privileges, all scripts on the same HTML page or layer must be signed. If you use layers, you can have both signed and unsigned scripts as long as you keep them in separate layers. For more information, see page 175.

You can sign JavaScript files (accessed with the SRC attribute of the <SCRIPT> tag), inline scripts, event handler scripts, and JavaScript entities. You cannot sign javascript: URLs. Before you sign the script, be sure you've properly identified it, as described in "Identifying Signed Scripts" on page 166.

USING PAGE SIGNER

Use ***Page Signer*** to sign scripts. Page Signer is a Perl script ("signPages") that uses **JAR Packager Command Line** to sign your scripts and package the digital signature and related information in a JAR file.

The signPages script extracts scripts from HTML files, signs them, and places their digital signatures in the archive specified by the ARCHIVE attribute in the <SCRIPT> tag from the HTML files. It also takes care of copying external JavaScript files loaded by the SRC attribute of the <SCRIPT> tag. The <SCRIPT> tags in the HTML pages can specify more than one JAR file; if so, signPages creates as many JAR files as it needs.

For information on using this tool, see page 161.

AFTER SIGNING

Once you've signed a script, any time you change it you must resign it. For JavaScript files, this means you cannot change anything in the file. For inline scripts, you cannot change anything between the initial <SCRIPT ...> and the closing </SCRIPT>. For event handlers and JavaScript entities, you cannot change anything at all in the tag that includes the handler or entity.

A change can be as simple as adding or removing whitespace in the script.

Changes to a signed script's byte stream invalidate the script's signature. This includes moving the HTML page between platforms that have different representations of text. For example, moving an HTML page from a Windows server to a UNIX server changes the byte stream and invalidates the signature. (This doesn't affect viewing pages from multiple platforms.) To avoid this, you can move the page in binary mode. Note that doing so changes the appearance of the page in your text editor but not in the browser.

Although you cannot make changes to the script, you can make changes to the surrounding information in the HTML file. You can even copy a signed script from one file to another, as long as you make sure you change nothing within the script.

TROUBLESHOOTING SIGNED SCRIPTS

Errors on the Java Console

If your signed scripts do not function as expected, be sure to check the Java console for errors. Errors may include the following:

```
# Error: Invalid Hash of this JAR entry (-7882)
# jar file: C:\Program
Files\Netscape\Users\norris\cache\MVI9CF1F.JAR
# path: 1
```

The path value printed for signed JavaScript is either the value of the ID attribute or the SRC attribute of the tag that supplied the script.

Debugging Invalid Hash Errors

Invalid hash errors occur if the script has changed from when it was signed. The most common cause of this problem is that the scripts have been moved from one platform to another with a text transfer rather than a binary transfer. Because line separator characters can differ from platform to platform, the hash could change from when the script was originally signed.

One good way to debug this sort of problem is to use the -s option to signPages, which will save the inline scripts in the JAR file. You can then unpack the jar file when you get the hash errors and compare it to the HTML file to track down the source of the problems. For information on signPages, see "Using Page Signer" on page 183.

"User did not grant privilege" Exception or Unsigned Script Dialog

Depending on whether or not you have enabled codebase principals, you see different behavior if a script attempts to enable privileges when it isn't signed or when its principals have been downgraded due to mixing.

If you have not enabled codebase principals and a script attempts to enable privileges for an unsigned script, it gets an exception from Java that the "user did not grant privilege". If you did enable codebase principals, you will see a Java security dialog that asking for permissions for the unsigned code.

This behavior is caused by either an error in verifying the certificate principals (which will cause an error to be printed to the Java console; see "Errors on the Java Console" on page 184), or by mixing signed and unsigned scripts. There are many possible sources of unsigned scripts. In particular, because there is no way to sign Javascript: URLs or dynamically generated scripts, using them causes the downgrading of principals.

SAMPLE SCRIPTS

Note: These sample scripts do not include complete HTML code for creating web pages, but they include <head> and <body> tags to indicate context for the JavaScript elements as well as any HTML code required to implement scripts, such as indicating the use of event handlers to call functions within element tags. JavaScript comments are used to identify the functionality of script components and HTML comments are used for notations regarding HTML syntax.

SCROLLING STATUS BAR MESSAGE

```
<head>
<script language=javascript>
<!-- Hide script from older browsers
/* This script places a scrolling message in the status bar
at the bottom of the browser window. The message includes
the current day, date and time. */
// MESSAGE TEXT
var input = "    "
input +="Greet visitors with a message that scrolls ";
input +="across the status bar at the bottom of the browser
window. . . ";
input +="            ";
var timer;
var msg = "";
// SCROLL FUNCTIONS
function scrollMaster() {
        msg = printDate(new Date())
        clearTimeout(timer)
        // CONCATENATE MESSAGE STRING
        msg += " " + showtime() + " " + input
        for (var i= 0; i < 100; i++){
                msg = " " + msg;
        }
        scrollText()
}
```

```
function scrollText(){
        window.status = msg;
        msg = msg.substring(1, msg.length) +
msg.substring(0,1);
        timer = setTimeout("scrollText()", 200);
}
// SHOW TIME FUNCTION
function showtime (){
        var now = new Date();
        var hours= now.getHours();
        var minutes= now.getMinutes();
        var seconds= now.getSeconds();
        var months= now.getMonth();
        var dates= now.getDate();
        var years= now.getYear();
        var timeValue = ""
                timeValue += ((months >9) ? "" : " ")
                timeValue += ((dates >9) ? "" : " ")
                timeValue = ( months +1)
                timeValue +="/"+ dates
                timeValue +="/"+  years
        var ap="A.M."
        if (hours == 12) {
                ap = "P.M."
        }
        if (hours == 0) {
                hours = 12
        }
        if(hours >= 13){
                hours -= 12;
                ap="P.M."
        }
        var timeValue2 = " " + hours
                timeValue2 += ((minutes < 10) ? ":0":":") +
                        minutes + " " + ap
        return timeValue2;
}
```

```
// MONTH AND DAY NAMES
function MakeArray(n) {
        this.length = n
        return this
}
monthNames = new MakeArray(12)
monthNames[0] = "Janurary"
monthNames[1] = "February"
monthNames[2] = "March"
monthNames[3] = "April"
monthNames[4] = "May"
monthNames[5] = "June"
monthNames[6] = "July"
monthNames[7] = "August"
monthNames[8] = "Sept."
monthNames[9] = "Oct."
monthNames[10] = "Nov."
monthNames[11] = "Dec."
daysNames = new MakeArray(7)
daysNames[0] = "Sunday"
daysNames[1] = "Monday"
daysNames[2] = "Tuesday"
daysNames[3] = "Wednesday"
daysNames[4] = "Thursday"
daysNames[5] = "Friday"
daysNames[6] = "Saturday"
```

```
// PRINT DAY-DATE FUNCTION
function printDate(oneDate) {
        var theDay = daysNames[oneDate.getDay()]
        var theDate =oneDate.getDate()
        var theMonth = monthNames[oneDate.getMonth()]
        var dayth="th"
        if ((theDate == 1) || (theDate == 21) || (theDate
== 31)) {
                dayth="st";
        }
        if ((theDate == 2) || (theDate ==22)) {
                dayth="nd";
        }
        if ((theDate== 3) || (theDate  == 23)) {
                dayth="rd";
        }
return theDay + ", " + theMonth + " " + theDate + dayth +
","
}
// Stop hiding -->
</script>
</head>


<!-- CALL SCROLL FUNCTION WITH EVENT HANDLER IN BODY TAG --
>
<body onload="scrollMaster()">
</body>
```

BASIC ROLLOVER

```
<head>
<script language=javascript>
<!-- Hide script from older browsers
/* This script causes one image to be replaced by another
when the pointer device moves over it. It also places a
message in the status bar when the pointing device button
is clicked. When the pointing devices moves away, the
original image is restored. */
// TEST BROWSER COMPATIBILITY AND PRELOAD IMAGES
if (document.images) {
        firstGraphic = new Image
        secondGraphic = new Image
        firstGraphic.src = 'firstGraphic.gif'
        secondGraphic.src = 'secondGraphic.gif'
}
else {
        firstGraphic = ""
        secondGraphic = ""
        document.graphic = ""
}
// Stop hiding -->
</script>
</head>
<body>
<!-- CALL SCRIPT WITH EVENTHANDLER IN LINK TAG -->
<A HREF="linked_page.html"
onmouseover="document.graphic.src=secondGraphic.src"
onmouseout="document.graphic.src=firstGraphic.src"
onmousedown="window.status='Display message in status
bar';return true">
<IMG SRC="firstGraphic.gif" NAME="graphic"></A>
</body>
```

CYCLING IMAGE DISPLAY

```
<head>

<script language=javascript>

<!-- Hide script from older browsers

/* This script automatically cycles through a series of
images at regular intervals, checking to make sure each
image has loaded completely before replacing it with the
next one. This is useful for cycling ad banners on a web
page or creating an automated slide show. */

// IDENTIFY IMAGES AND SET COUNTER

var cycleGraphics = new
Array("picture1.gif","picture2.gif","picture3.gif")

var thisGraphic = 0

var imgCt = 3

// CYCLE FUNCTION

function imageCycle() {

        // TEST FOR OLDER BROWSERS

        if (document.images) {

                // TEST FOR IMAGE LOADING

                if (document.featureGraphic.complete) {

                        // INCREMENT OR RESET COUNTER

                        thisGraphic++

                        if (thisGraphic == imgCt) {

                                thisGraphic = 0

                        }

                        // REPLACE IMAGE WITH NEXT GRAPHIC IN ARRAY

document.featureGraphic.src=cycleGraphics[thisGraphic]

                }

                // SET CYCLE TIME

                setTimeout("imageCycle()", 5 * 1000)

        }

}
```

```
// Stop hiding -->
</script>
</head>

<!-- CALL FUNCTION WITH EVENT HANDLER IN BODY TAG -->
<body onload="imageCycle()">
<!-- IDENTIFY CYCLING OBJECT WITH NAME PROPERTY IN IMAGE TAG -->
<img src="picture1.gif" name="featureGraphic">
</body>
```

RANDOM IMAGE DISPLAY

```
<head>
<script language=javascript>
<!-- Hide script from older browsers
/* This script displays an image selected at random from a
specified array. */
// IDENTIFY IMAGES
var displayPix = new
Array("image1.gif","image2.gif","image3.jpg")
// SELECTION FUNCTION
function chooseImg() {
        if (document.images) {
                // GENERATE RANDOM NUMBER BETWEEN 0 AND 2
                randomNum = Math.floor((Math.random() * 10)) % 3
                document.myDisplay.src = displayPix[randomNum]
        }
}
// --> Stop hiding
</script>
</head>
<!-- CALL FUNCTION WITH EVENT HANDLER IN BODY TAG -->
<body onload="chooseImg()">
<!-- IDENTIFY DISPLAY OBJECT WITH NAME PROPERTY IN IMAGE TAG -->
<img src="image1.gif" name="myDisplay">
</body>
```

INTERACTIVE SLIDE SHOW

```
<head>

<script language=javascript>

<!-- Hide script from older browsers

/* This script allows the viewer to move back and forth
through as series of slides */

// IDENTIFY SLIDE IMAGES AND SET COUNTER

var mySlides = new
Array("image1.gif","image2.gif","image3.gif")

var thisSlide = 0

// DEFINE BACKWARD NAVIGATION FUNCTION

function moveBack() {
        if (document.images && thisSlide > 0) {
                thisSlide--
                document.myShow.src=mySlides[thisSlide]
        }
}

// DEFINE FORWARD NAVIGATION FUNCTION

function moveAhead() {
        if (document.images && thisSlide < 2) {
                thisSlide++
                document.myShow.src=mySlides[thisSlide]
        }
}

// --> Stop hiding

</script>

</head>

<body>

<!-- CREATE SLIDE SHOW OBJECT WITH NAME PROPERTY IN IMAGE TAG -->

<img src="image1.gif" name="myShow">

<!-- CALL FUNCTION FROM LINK -->

<a href=javascript:moveBack()>Back</a>

<a href=javascript:moveAhead()>Forward</a>

</body>
```

PREVENTING FRAME CAPTURE

```
<head>

<script language=javascript>

<!-- Hide script from older browsers

/* This script forces a page to display in a new browser
window instead of being captured in a frame by a link from
a frameset environment. */

<script>

if (top.location != self.location) {

       top.location = self.location

}

// --> Stop hiding

</script>

</head>
```

FORCING A FRAMESET INTO A FRAME

```
<head>

<script language=javascript>

<!-- Hide script from older browsers

/* This script forces an entire frameset to display even when
a user accesses a specific frame from an external link */

<script>

if (top.location == self.location {

       top location.href="frameset.html"

}

// --> Stop hiding

</script>

</head>
```

WRITING CONTENT TO ANOTHER FRAME

```
<head>

<script language=javascript>

<!-- Hide script from older browsers

/* This script writes a new HTML page to a frame named
"target" when a the user selects a link. */

<script>

function writeContent(apples) {

       parent.target.document.write("<html><head></
head><body bgcolor=white><h1>")

parent.target.document.write("Do you really want "+apples+
apples?")

parent.target.document.write("</h1></body></html>")

parent.target.document.close()

}

// --> Stop hiding

</script>

</head>

<body>

How many apples would you like?<br><br>

<!--CALL FUNCTION AND PASS VALUE TO SCRIPT WHEN LINK IS SELECTED-->

<a href="javascript:writeContent(2)">2 apples</a>

<a href="javascript:writeContent(3)">3 apples</a>

<a href="javascript:writeContent(4)">4 apples</a>

</body>
```

VALIDATING EMAIL ADDRESS

```
<head>

<script language=javascript>

<!-- Hide script from older browsers

/* This script checks user input on a form to ensure that
data has been properly entered. */

// TEST USER INPUT

function validData(email) {

        // DEFINE INVALID CHARACTERS

        invalidChars = " /:,;"

        // TEST FOR CONTENT

        if (email=="") {

                return false

        }

        // TEST FOR INVALID CHARACTERS

        for (i=0; i<invalidChars.length;i++) {

        badChar = invalidChars.charAt(i)

                if (email.indexOf(badChar,0) != -1) {

                        return false

                }

        }

        // TEST FOR UNIQUE @ CHARACTER

        atPos = email.indexOf("@",1)

        if (atPos == -1) {

                return false

        }

        if (email.indexOf("@",atPos+1) != -1) {

                return false

        }

        // TEST FOR DOT

        dotPos = email.indexOf(".",atPos)
```

```
        if (dotPos <= 0) {
                return false
        }
        if (dotPos+3 > email.length) {
                return false
        }
        return true
}
// VALIDATE AND SUBMIT
function submitData(form) {
        if (!validEmail(form.emailAddr.value)) {
                alert("Invalid email address")
                form.emailAddr.focus()
                form.emailAddr.select()
                return false
        }
        return true
}
// --> Stop hiding
</script>
</head>
<body>
<!-- CALL SCRIPT WITH EVENT HANDLER -->
<form name="formName" onSubmit="return
submitForm(formName);" method="post" action="mailto.cgi">
<!-- LINK EMAIL DATA TO SCRIPT WITH NAME PROPERTY -->
Email <input type="text" name="emailAddr">
<input type="submit" name="submit">
</form>
</body>
```

REQUIRING A MENU CHOICE

```
<head>

<script language=javascript>

<!-- Hide script from older browsers

/* This script checks an input field on a form and alerts
users if they fail to make a selection for that field. */

function submitData(form) {

        userChoice = form.menuName.selectedIndex

        if (form.menuName.options[userChoice].value == "")
{

                alert("You must make a selection")

                return false

        }

        return true

}

// --> Stop hiding

</script>

</head>

<body>

<!-- CALL SCRIPT WITH EVENT HANDLER IN FORM TAG -->

<form name="formName" onSubmit="return
submitData(formName);" method="post" action="mailto.cgi">

<p>

<!-- LINK FIELD TO SCRIPT WITH NAME PROPERTY -->

Choose something: <select name="menuName">
        <option value="" selected>options
        <option value="apples">Apples
        <option value="peaches">Peaches
        <option value="pumpkin pie">Pumpkin Pie
        </select>

<p>

<input type="submit" name="submit" value="That's it!">

</form>

</body>
```

OPENING A NEW WINDOW

```
<head>

<script language=javascript>

<!-- Hide script from older browsers

/* This script opens a new browser window with specified
properties and content. */

function newWindow() {

       detailWindow =
           window.open('image.jpeg','windowName',
           'scrollbars=yes,width=250,height=350')

}

// --> Stop hiding

</script>

</head>

<body>

<!-- CALL FUNCTION IN LINK TAG -->

<a href="javascript:newWindow()">Example</a>

</body>
```

COOKIE FORMAT

```
cookieName=cookieValue;

expires=expirationDateGMT; path=URLpath;

domain=siteDomain
```

DOWNLOADABLE SCRIPTS AND TIPS

Selected examples of code from ASP publications are available for free downloading from the ASP website. Now you can study and customize these programs without tedious keyboarding.

Visit <**www.aspinc.com**> and click on the "Downloads" icon. After entering basic registration information, you will be taken to the Download Requests page where you may choose examples from a variety of ASP publications.

QUICK REFERENCE PUBLICATIONS FROM ASP

UNIX Quick Reference Guide

You don't need to fumble through oversized volumes for quick reference lookups. Get a concise reference guide to UNIX in a single, compact handbook. The ***UNIX Quick Reference Guide*** contains the user and many admin commands for UNIX, including Solaris and BSD, plus hundreds of examples.

Bourne Shell Quick Reference Guide

The Bourne Shell was the original shell for UNIX, and it still remains the most widely used and distributed. The ***Bourne Shell Quick Reference Guide*** summarizes this scripting language and includes complete sample programs and examples. Many UNIX commands used in Bourne Shell scripting are also included.

C Shell Quick Reference Guide

The C Shell was developed as a replacement for the standard Bourne shell and is found on most systems running UNIX. The ***C Shell Quick Reference Guide*** covers this scripting language and includes complete sample programs and examples. Many UNIX commands used in C Shell scripting are also included.

Korn Shell Quick Reference Guide

The Korn Shell is an interactive command and programming language that provides an interface to UNIX and other systems. The ***Korn Shell Quick Reference Guide*** covers all aspects of the Korn Shell, with complete Korn shell scripts and many examples included.

Tcl Quick Reference Guide

The ***Tcl Quick Reference Guide*** covers the Tool Control Language and includes complete sample programs and practical examples.

Quick Reference Cards

Vi, C, C++, SCCS, HTML Reference Cards

Multi-fold cards provide concise summaries for programmers and users.

For order information, email books@aspinc.com